Instructor's Manual

The Art of
Reasoning

Instructor's Manual

The Art of
Reasoning

David Kelley

W · W · Norton & Company   New York London

Printed in the United States of America

First Edition

W. W. Norton & Company, Inc.
500 Fifth Ave, New York, NY 10110

W. W. Norton & Company Ltd.
37 Great Russell Street, London WC1B 3NU

ISBN 0-393-95615-6

1 2 3 4 5 6 7 8 9 0

CONTENTS

CONTENTS

CHAPTER 1

INTRODUCTION

Like an Auxiliary in Plato's <u>Republic</u>, a textbook writer should know his place. The most important tasks in a course on critical reasoning should be left to the instructor, because they require a judgment about the particular problems, strengths, and interests of the students. A textbook should free the instructor to concentrate on those tasks by taking care of more routine matters and providing a stock of resources for the instructor to use. This conception of the division of labor underlies the major features of <u>The Art of Reasoning</u>.

As with the acquisition of any ability, students in critical thinking must learn a set of component skills—isolating premises and conclusions, detecting fallacies, assessing deductive validity and inductive strength—and they must learn how to integrate these skills so that they can handle "real life" material in a comprehensive and flexible way. They must learn to serve, hit forehand and backhand, but they must also learn to orchestrate these skills in playing an actual game of tennis. In my view, the task of integration falls primarily on the instructor's side of the division of labor. It requires work on actual examples, with students getting feedback that a book cannot provide. And instructors who agree on individual tactics in argument analysis (find the conclusion, check for fallacies, etc.) often disagree on how to assemble them into global strategies. I have therefore tried to cover the component topics independently, in a basically modular way, so that instructors have as much freedom as possible in choosing which ones to cover, in what order, in what degree of depth. Though I make a greater effort than most modular texts to provide integrating links among topics, these take the form of a web of connections rather than a rigid architectonic structure.

I have also tried to present the material in a clear, engaging, and conversational style, so that students will actually do the reading and come to class prepared, and instructors will not have to spend time reviewing the basics. In this connection, I have kept the theoretical material to a minimum, including only those points necessary to make the practical techniques and rules intelligible. In some cases, such as the relation between explanation and argument, the theoretical issues are controversial, and I wanted to minimize the amount of time an instructor must spend "arguing with the text." Even where issues are not controversial, students vary a good deal in their ability and appetite for theory, so I felt the choice to include it should be left to the instructor. In my comments on each chapter, I will indicate some of the issues which I decided not to raise but which might be raised in class.

To some extent, of course, the book does reflect my own theoretical preferences, and I will try to identify these as well. One pedagogical thesis is worth mentioning here. In my experience, many beginning students have not had much training in the mechanics of language, or developed the habit of attending to differences in the meanings of words and statements. In addition, they often lack any clear sense of what an argument is, or why it is necessary to back up an assertion with reasons; they seem to regard all opinions as on a par, either as self-evident or as subjective matters of taste. But once they get the point of analyzing language and giving arguments, I find they can usually make rapid progress. For this reason, Parts III and IV proceed at a somewhat faster pace than Parts I and II.

The book includes more material than can easily be covered in a single semester-length course, even at the brisk pace of a chapter a week, and some selection will therefore be necessary. The modular design allows for various choices. It would be possible to cover just Parts I and II (Chapters 1-7), with the first section of Chapter 14 (Using Statistics in Argument) and Chapter 15 (Explanation) perhaps included as well. This would be particularly appropriate if the course includes a writing component, or if the instructor wants to supplement the chapters on argument with longer passages for more extended analysis. On the other hand, if one has more advanced students and wishes to emphasize the more technical material, it would be possible to concentrate on Parts III and IV, omitting much of the first half of the book. Between these extremes lie many possibilities, made possible by the fact that within each Part, later chapters can be omitted without losing the value of earlier ones. This Manual is intended to help make these choices by summarizing briefly the contents of each chapter, and by indicating what earlier material it presupposes.

I have not made any suggestions about how much material to cover in a single class session. Course schedules and student ability vary too much for any recommendations to be useful. The chapters are structured to allow for such variety. Each one is divided into sections, with most sections followed by Practice Quizzes. Some of the Exercises at the end of the chapter, moreover, test students on material in specific sections, so that they can be used even if one has not completed the chapter (in my comments on each exercise, I indicate which sections they presuppose).

For the Practice Quizzes, I have tried to select items that have a definitely right or at least preferred answer, though in some cases there is bound to be dispute. I have adjusted the difficulty and length of the quizzes so that they will take the average student 15–30 minutes, and will provide a test of his understanding of the section. To aid in this self-diagnostic function, I have included the answers in the back of the book. This should allow students to come to class with fairly definite questions about material they don't understand (and perhaps with definite objections to my answers).

The Exercises at the end of each chapter are extensive. Most instructors will probably not want to use all of them; my intent was to provide a resource allowing as much freedom of choice as possible. Though some of these exercises could be assigned as homework, I expect their primary use will be for in-class work, as a means of practicing and integrating the material covered in the text, under the guidance of the instructor. The Exercises are more difficult than the Practice Quizzes, and most of them have more than one "right" answer, or at least require discussion and the use of judgment to select the best among plausible alternatives. I have included creative exercises requiring students to come up with their own

definitions, arguments, and explanations as well as
critical exercises asking them to evaluate those of
others. In the critical types of exercise, I have
drawn passages from works in many different
disciplines, so that most students will encounter
material from subjects that interest them, material
which they may even have studied in other courses.
Different exercises ask students to use the same
skills in different tasks, with the goal of
maintaining student interest and helping students
acquire flexibility in the use of the skills. In
addition, some of the exercises are integrative,
asking students to combine material from different
chapters.

Though this Manual will include comments on the
text of each chapter, it is intended primarily as a
user's guide to the end of chapter exercises. I will
indicate what portions of the text are presupposed by
each exercise, make suggestions for the use of each
exercise, and provide the answers that seem most
natural to me. It should go without saying that my
answers are presented as points of departure for
discussion and debate, not as the final word.

CHAPTER 2

CLASSIFICATION

Contents

Concepts and Referents: species and genus as logical terms; recognizing different levels of abstraction.

Rules of Classification: mutually exclusive and jointly exhaustive classifications; using a single principle or set of principles consistently; classifying by essential principles.

Levels of Organization: organizing newly learned concepts into hierarchies of species and genus; distinguishing part/whole from species/genus relationships.

Classification and Outlining: applying the rules to the process of outlining a term paper; no Practice Quiz.

Comments

The material in this chapter is very basic, but it can be covered quickly and has a high payoff. Some students seem to treat all concepts as atomic, self-contained units, and lack any clear sense of the relations of class inclusion or the existence of different levels of abstraction; and even good students benefit from the exercises in the third section. Students who master this material find it easier to understand categorical syllogisms, inductive generalizations, and statistical reasoning.

In the second section, I present the requirements that a classification be mutually exclusive, jointly exhaustive, and based on a single principle as a single rule rather than as three. Here, as throughout the book, I have tried to reduce the information load on students by giving them the fewest number of units to remember, and it seemed to me that these three points could legitimately be viewed as aspects of a single rule.

The rule that one should classify by essential principles raises a host of issues about essences. My own view is that essentiality is a matter of degree, and that it is determined <u>both</u> by the facts about the set of objects being classified <u>and</u> by the context of our knowledge about those objects and our cognitive purposes. But the rule is presented in such a way that those with a more realist view on the one hand, or a more conventionalist view on the other, can interpret the rule accordingly.

The final section, on the use of classification in outlining a writing project, is an appendix that can be assigned or omitted as one chooses; nothing else in the book depends on it.

EXERCISE A. Presupposes the first section but not the second or third.

1. Sauntered, strode,...
2. Turned,...; glass, goblet,...
3. Almost any laudatory term would do. This might be an occasion for observing how vague and undiscriminating "nice" is, and how little information it conveys.
4. Country, domain (notice the different assumptions behind these terms); quadruped, animal
5. Passionately (more specific in terms of degree of feeling), angrily (more specific in terms of kind of feeling),...
6. Dream, illusion
7. Institution
8. Problem, anxiety, hatred: same point here as in 3.
9. Perilous, deadly
10. Countless, a huge number, 57,...

EXERCISE B. Presupposes the second section but not the third.

1. Could classify by part of body covered (shoes, socks, shirts, etc.), by degree of formality (sports clothes, office dress, evening wear, etc.). Consider where nontypical clothing would fit: uniforms, togas, etc.
2. Names of appliances (stove, refrigerator, vacuum cleaner) already embody a classification by function. Students should be asked to provide higher-order groupings--e.g., appliances for storing and

preparing food, personal hygiene, cleaning house, etc.
Contrast with classification by source of power:
electric, gas, etc.

   3. Could classify by content (current affairs,
academic subjects, reference material, etc.) and by
format (periodical vs. nonperiodical), with
subdivisions within each. It's worth doing both, since
both principles normally must be used in defining any
particular type.

   4. Could classify by geographical area, type of
government, level of development. This is a good
example to illustrate the cognitive effects of
classification. Compare the stereotypes invoked by
labelling country X as African, communist, Third
World.

   5. The standard and most essential division is
probably by type of function performed: manual,
clerical, managerial, sales, etc. Alternatives: type
of industry, type of ability required, typical salary
ranges. One might ask students which principle they
use in thinking about their choice of careers.

EXERCISE C. Presupposes the third section

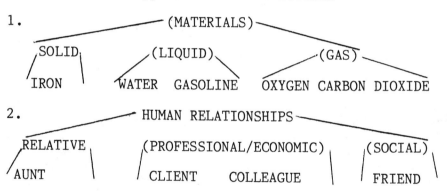

[One could treat relatives and social relationships as
species of PERSONAL RELATIONSHIPS, putting the latter
on the same level as PROFESSIONAL/ECONOMIC.]

3.

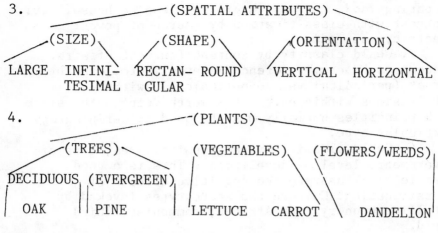

(SPATIAL ATTRIBUTES)

(SIZE) (SHAPE) (ORIENTATION)

LARGE INFINI- RECTAN- ROUND VERTICAL HORIZONTAL
       TESIMAL GULAR

4.

(PLANTS)

(TREES) (VEGETABLES) (FLOWERS/WEEDS)

DECIDUOUS (EVERGREEN)

OAK PINE LETTUCE CARROT DANDELION

[Compare this ordinary language, layman's system with the biological classification.]

5.

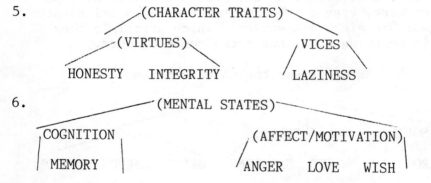

(CHARACTER TRAITS)

(VIRTUES) VICES

HONESTY INTEGRITY LAZINESS

6.

(MENTAL STATES)

COGNITION (AFFECT/MOTIVATION)

MEMORY ANGER LOVE WISH

[One might want to subdivide affective states further into emotions, as responses to things and events (passions in the classical sense), and desires, as impulses to action; with anger and love as types of emotion, and wish as a type of desire. One might also compare (5) and (6), observing different principles at work in classifying traits and states.]

EXERCISE D. Presupposes the second section, and the more difficult ones (5 & 6) require the third. Though the exercise does not ask students to evaluate the classifications, this might be a topic for discussion.

1.

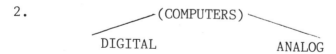

HUMAN BEINGS

BORROWERS   LENDERS

[One might ask students how many other "There are two kinds of people" jokes they've heard.]

2.

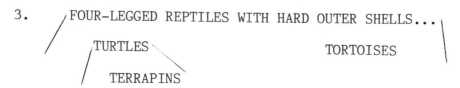

(COMPUTERS)

DIGITAL   ANALOG

3.

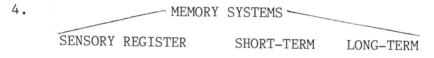

FOUR-LEGGED REPTILES WITH HARD OUTER SHELLS...

TURTLES   TORTOISES

TERRAPINS

[This is a confusing passage because it isn't clear how the description "four-legged reptiles..." relates to the biological orders mentioned.]

4.

MEMORY SYSTEMS

SENSORY REGISTER   SHORT-TERM   LONG-TERM

[Another possibility would be to treat sensory registers and memory systems as contrasting categories, with long- and short-term memory as a further subdivision; but I think the arrangement I have is more in keeping with the passage as written.]

5.

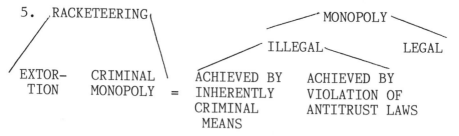

RACKETEERING   MONOPOLY

                       ILLEGAL   LEGAL

| EXTOR-TION | CRIMINAL MONOPOLY = | ACHIEVED BY INHERENTLY CRIMINAL MEANS | ACHIEVED BY VIOLATION OF ANTITRUST LAWS |

[This is a tricky one because the author is locating criminal monopoly within two genuses, but this is a common mode of analysis.]

6.

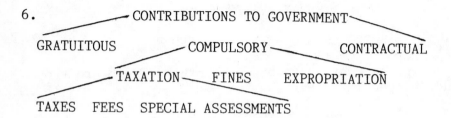

CONTRIBUTIONS TO GOVERNMENT

GRATUITOUS   COMPULSORY   CONTRACTUAL

TAXATION   FINES   EXPROPRIATION

TAXES   FEES   SPECIAL ASSESSMENTS

EXERCISE E. Presupposes the second section but not the third (unless one goes on to devise an alternative system). If one's own school has an analogous classification, I strongly recommend using it in place of this one. It's a great motivator for students to realize that they can use logic to evaluate the system in which they find themselves. If one does use the system in the text, some questions to ask:

Why is English separated from other literatures?

Why is Physical Education an Art?

How can Computer Science be a natural science?

Why is Psychology a natural rather than a social science?

Why are Philosophy and Religion social sciences?

CHAPTER 3

DEFINITION

Contents

The Functions of a Definition: introductory material on the value of defining; no Practice Quiz.

Rules for Definitions: the classical Aristotelian rules for definition by genus and differentia, with emphasis on the cognitive rationale for each rule.

Constructing Definitions: additional considerations on using the rules to construct definitions; extended discussion of defining GAME as an example.

Comments

Chapter 2 provides a natural background and preparation for this chapter, but this one could be used without having covered Chapter 2 if one explains the terms genus and species.

Beyond an occasional mention, I do not discuss stipulative definitions. They are used mainly in technical areas, and students will learn what they need to know in the course of technical training. But it might be worth mentioning that if a term is introduced and defined by stipulation, there is no need to consider whether it is too narrow or too broad.

On the rule that a definition should include essential attributes, see the comment on essentiality in the previous chapter.

EXERCISE A: Presupposes the second section. The third section would help with part (b) but is not necessary, since students are not being asked to define the terms from scratch, but only to fix errors.

1. a) Too narrow; nonessential. b) An army is the branch of a country's military whose primary function is to fight on land.

2. a) Too narrow (table lamps, outdoor hurricane lamps); too broad (candle). b) A lamp is an enclosed

light source that is movable but not designed to be carried on one's person. [The idea here is to locate lamps on a spectrum of portability between wall or ceiling fixtures on the one hand, and flashlights, headlights, etc., on the other. As with many other terms for artifacts, this is a good one for discussing borderline cases.]

3. a) No genus; too broad (arm-wrestling). b) A handshake is a social gesture in which two people clasp each other's right hand.

4. a) Circular. b) A genus is the broader class to which the referents of a given concept belong.

5. a) Too broad (injuries); nonessential. b) A disease is a condition of an organism involving the malfunction of one or more parts in a way that threatens the organism's health.

6. a) Nonessential. Too broad if taken literally (some tasks would be easy for anyone). b) A craftsman is a person who is skilled at creating a specific type of product. [One might argue that craftsmanship should not be limited to specific products, but should apply to any skill or talent; I consider that a metaphorical extension, but the point is certainly debatable.]

7. a) Too broad (everyone is fooled occasionally). b) A gullible person is a person who can easily be fooled.

8. a) Negative. b) Thinking is purposeful mental activity whose goal is acquiring knowledge or understanding.

9. a) Too broad (all the social sciences would be included). Too narrow (animal studies would be excluded). b) Psychology is the science that studies the functioning of the mind. [Theorists of many different schools could accept this definition by interpreting "functioning" and "mind" in different ways, but the definition is still somewhat tendentious. I don't know of a perfectly neutral one; this might be an occasion for discussing the point about not putting controversial claims into a definition.]

10. a) Negative. b) A condominium is an individually owned unit in a multi-unit residential building.

11. a) Too narrow (a person can reform). b) To reform is to improve a person or organization by

changing the principles on which the person or organization acts. [The term "principles" must be taken pretty broadly here to include character, personality, and beliefs in the case of persons; and laws, policies, and structure in the case of organizations.]

12. a) Circular. Too narrow (executive branch of government). b) An executive is a person or agency responsible for putting a policy into effect.

EXERCISE B. Presupposes the second section. This exercise has a standard "name the rule violated" format, and thus duplicates Exercises A and C. I include it because the difference between serious and humorous definitions is not obvious to some students. All of these would be nonessential as stated, and either too broad or too narrow. Most are also metaphorical. I would suggest focusing discussion on other rules violated--no genus: (2) and (5); negative: (1) and (10). One might also discuss what gives each quip its bite, and consider whether the point would be included somehow in a proper definition.

EXERCISE C. Presupposes the second section.
1. Too broad.
2. Vague, too broad.
3. This is certainly too broad if one accepts an absolute rather than a relative concept of poverty, a possible topic for discussion. Which concept is appropriate for social scientists? historians? policy makers? Even on relative conception, the words "customary" and "widely encouraged and approved" may make this too broad, or too vague.
4. Too broad.
5. This seems adequate to me, so long as one treats "crimes against nature (or nature's Law)," "crimes against humanity," etc. as metaphorical extensions.
6. Too broad. If frankness is a trait, as opposed to the action expressing the trait, this also lacks the right genus.
7. Vague, nonessential.
8. This seems basically adequate to me, though the language makes it vulnerable to the charge of vagueness. One might discuss whether terms like

"common will" and "established forms" might be given more precise substitutes.

    9. Metaphorical.

    10. The absence of any reference to goal, purpose, or function may make this nonessential.

    11. Negative.

    12. Vague. The word "command" also suggests a Baconian view; those who see scientific knowledge as an end in itself would regard this as too narrow and nonessential.

    13. Nonessential: a definition should state the action or function of regulating, not the legal genesis of the authority to perform the action.

    14. This seems adequate to me. I would put in a plug for dictionaries here.

    15. This seems adequate if taken in a normative sense, as describing the official, justifying distinction between a tax and a fee or special assessment (see Seligman's classification, Chapter 2, Exercise D, 6). Obviously some tax money is in fact used to benefit special interests.

EXERCISE D. Presupposes the third section. In my experience, students have trouble coming up with their own definitions until they are willing to distinguish literal from metaphorical uses of a term. The point of this exercise is to encourage that distinction.

    1. (b) is clearly a metaphorical extension, deriving from "headshrinker."

    2. Different concepts: in (a), "party" refers to an event involving entertainment; in (b), it refers to a group of people acting as a unit in a social or legal context.

    3. Same concept: an action performed on an object to discover its properties, abilities, or tendencies.

    4. (b) and (c) seem to involve the same concept: an external force that threatens a thing's internal structure or functioning. (If force is regarded as something inherently physical, then (b) would be a metaphorical extension of (c).) (a) is a synonym for "emphasize," at best a metaphorical extension of the concept.

    5. Since "revolution" in (a) can be given a physical definition not applicable to social events, I would say (b) involves a different concept, though it

may originally have been a metaphorical extension.
(c) involves a metaphorical extension or exaggeration
of (b).

EXERCISE E. Presupposes the third section and Chapter
2. This is an integrative exercise designed to show
how terms within a classification hierarchy can be
interdefined.

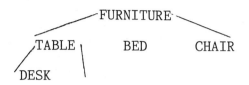

FURNITURE: movable man-made objects designed to
support and/or store other objects.
TABLE: an article of furniture designed with the
primary purpose of supporting other objects on a flat
and rigid top surface.
BED: an article of furniture with a horizontal surface
designed to support a sleeper.
CHAIR: an article of furniture designed to support a
sitting or reclining person on a horizontal surface,
with a vertical surface to support the back.
DESK: a table designed for work by a seated person,
with a flat surface to support working materials and
drawers or pigeonholes to store them.

EXERCISE F. Presupposes the third section. If this is
done in class, I would suggest dividing students into
working groups of 3-5 if possible.
    1. BACHELOR: an unmarried adult human male.
    2. DIFFERENTIA: the part of a definition that
distinguishes the referents of a concept from other
species of the same genus.
    3. BORROW: to take temporary possession of
something belonging to another, with a promise to
return it or its equivalent according to an
agreement.
    4. COMPUTER: a device for processing information
according to an alterable set of instructions.
    5. OBEY: to act in accordance with and on the
basis of a rule or command. [This presupposes that the
"obedience" of a stone to the law of gravity reflects

a different concept or a metaphorical extension, a
debatable point.]

    6. JOURNALISM: the activity of gathering and
disseminating information about current events of
significance to a given audience.

    7. NOVICE: a person who is relatively unskilled
in a given activity.

    8. JEALOUSY: the emotion a) of resentment toward
another person for possessing something [including
things, attributes, relationships] that one wants or
feels entitled to, or b) of obsessive fear of losing
to another what one possesses. [This one is especially
hard, as every element in the definition is debatable.
I would put special emphasis here on having students
begin by locating jealousy in a classification scheme,
relating it to anger, resentment, envy, indignation,
etc.]

EXERCISE G. Presupposes the second section, but the
third would help. This is a very open-ended exercise
for discussion. I would emphasize the role of
political views and allegiances in choosing a
definition, and the potential for people of opposing
views to talk past each other. Points to consider:

    VIOLENCE is the genus in every definition but
(2), which mentions various types of violence. Which
is preferable?

    One differentia pertains to the perpetrator and
the victims. Can governments commit terrorism? (1)-(3)
seem to allow this, (4) and (5) to deny it. The
victims must be civilians in (3), the innocent in (2),
the public in (1) and (4); (5) does not include
anything on this point.

    Another differentia is the purpose of the
violence: political goals (1 and 2); political or
social (4); political or religious (5). Which is the
best choice? (3) makes no reference to specific goals;
does this allow criminal gangs to count as terrorists?
Should they?

EXERCISE H. Presupposes the chapter as a whole, as
well as Chapter 2. This exercise is not as directly
related as the other ones to logical skills, but it
can be an eye-opener for students who have never been
asked to defend their word choices in writing.

1. Both are types of recreation, but reflect subdivisions of the genus by different principles of classification: games are distinguished by rules from less structured activities; sports are distinguished by their physical character from less strenuous activities.

2. All three involve a willingness to undergo danger; various plausible distinctions could be drawn among them. "Brave" and "courageous" may be synonyms, with boldness either a species distinguished by eagerness or excitement at the risk, or an attribute distinguished from courage as in Aristotle's Ethics. Alternatively, "brave" might be considered the generic term, with courage and boldness considered species: courage is bravery that results from an understanding of and commitment to the values at stake; boldness from eagerness for excitement.

3. "Hurt" is the most general term, since it includes physical as well as emotional injury. Restricted to emotional injury, it seems to overlap with "offense." To hurt is to act in a way that causes pain or sorrow to another; to offend is to act in a way that violates a moral norm or denigrates the values of another; one may be hurt by actions that are not offensive and be offended by actions that don't hurt. An insult seems to be a species of offense, distinguished by being deliberate and (possibly) by its verbal form.

4. All three terms indicate a person's tendency—more or less deliberate and more or less habitual—to make his overt actions reflect his inner beliefs and feelings. "Sincere" is normally used for nonverbal actions and displays of feeling, "honest" for verbal ones, with frankness perhaps best seen as a species of honesty distinguished by the bluntness of the expression or the unpleasantness of what is expressed.

5. All three are forms of teaching. "Instruct" seems the most general term, with "educate" normally restricted to the kinds of skills and bodies of knowledge taught in schools and "train" restricted to technical, physical or vocational skills.

6. "Idealist" might be considered the generic term, indicating loyalty and commitment to a cause, with "crusader" a species distinguished by activism in

pursuit of the cause, and "zealot" a subspecies distinguished by irrationality in the commitment and/or insensitivity in the pursuit.

7. Two possibilities: 1) To adorn is to make a person more visually pleasing, to decorate is to make a nonhuman object more pleasing, with "garnish" either a synonym or a subcategory restricted to food. 2) To adorn is to add to the visual attraction of something that is already pleasing in itself, to decorate is to make pleasing something that in itself is plain or unattractive, with "garnish" as in (1).

8. All three involve a thing's power to cause desire or positive feeling in a person. "Attractive" seems the generic term. Both "seductive" and "tempting" are limited to cases where the thing causes a desire that would be expressed in a more or less specific type of action; "seductive" carries the implication that the action would be wrong (or be considered wrong, unseemly, risque by some standard), and may thus be considered a subspecies.

EXERCISE I. These are intended for courses that devote some attention to writing skills. In (1) I would have students revise their first efforts, cutting out some number of words; or have them edit each others' efforts. In (2), I would have students work in pairs, with each responsible for checking the other's telegram to make sure it is intelligible.

CHAPTER 4

PROPOSITIONS

Contents

Propositions and Sentences: propositions as statements that must be true or false; subject-predicate structure of simple declarative sentences. No Practice Quiz.

Propositions and Word Meaning: using techniques of classification and definition to tell whether words are synonomous; connotation vs. literal meaning; interpreting metaphors.

Propositions and Grammar: grammatical devices for asserting more than one proposition in a sentence; restrictive vs. nonrestrictive clauses; conjunctions; noun clauses.

Comments

This chapter is intended to serve as a preparation for argument analysis. Students often have trouble isolating premises and conclusions because they lack a clear concept of propositions as units of thought and assertion, and have trouble distinguishing among different propositions; the point of the chapter is to sharpen these skills. The ground covered in the chapter is a minefield of issues in the philosophy of language. I have tried to concentrate on material that is most helpful to students and least controversial theoretically. Those who skip the chapter because of disagreements with the text might still find some value in the exercises.

Despite the value of this chapter in preparing for argument analysis, the later chapters do not explicitly presuppose it. The chapter could also be used without having done Chapters 2 and 3 if one does a little filling in at the beginning of the second section. Within the chapter, the third section could be covered even if one skips the second.

In the second section, I use the term "connotation" in the literary sense most students learn in high school—the emotional flavor and images associated with a word--not the philosophical sense in which it is roughly equivalent to "intension." I do not discuss the connotation/denotation or intension/extension distinction a) because I oppose it on theoretical grounds, and b) because I do not think it would have great pedagogical value even if true. Those who disagree, however, can easily introduce it within the framework established by the chapters on classification and definition.

In the third section I distinguish between propositions that are asserted in a sentence and those that are expressed but not asserted (e.g., antecedent and consequent in hypothetical propositions). I do not know of any _general_ rule for distinguishing asserted from nonasserted propositions. If students ask about this, I would say that a sentence asserts any proposition it expresses unless some specific device suspends assertion; being asserted is the default condition.

In determining which propositions a sentence asserts, there is a slippery slope from the sentence itself, as a whole, to the full list of states of affairs that must obtain for the sentence to be true. Without a canonical way of regimenting statements in natural language, distinguishing atomic from compound statements, and formulating truth conditions, I don't know of any alternative but to rely on common sense judgments about what a speaker has stated more or less explicitly.

EXERCISE A. Presupposes the second and third sections, though it could be done just on the basis of one or the other. Each answer below is of course only one among many possibilities.

1. Joanne met Bob for lunch.
2. The dog fell asleep on the sofa.
3. Rain today is unlikely.
4. John bought his stereo at half price.
5. Shakespeare was a poet and Shakespeare was a playwright.
6. Although _Out of Africa_ was a good movie, the pace was too slow.
7. The mail will not be delivered on Wednesday because it is a holiday.

8. Men are not created unequal.

9. I will be able to see my family more often if I move to Chicago, where they live.

10. I don't accept John Calvin's statement that people are innately evil.

EXERCISE B. Presupposes the third section. To save space, I have listed only the component propositions, and not repeated the sentence as a whole. The examples could also be used to introduce the topic of compatible vs. incompatible propositions.

1. A pedestrian hit me (a).
   A pedestrian went under my car (a).
2. I collided with a truck (a).
   The truck was stationary (a).
   The truck was coming the other way (a).
3. I pulled away from the left side of the road (a).
   I glanced at my mother-in-law (a).
   I headed over the embankment (a).
4. The pedestrian had no idea which direction to go (a).
   I ran over the pedestrian (a).
5. I approached the intersection (a).
   A stop sign suddenly appeared in a place (a).
   No stop sign had ever appeared in that place before (a).
6. I was not injured (e).
   I told the police that I was not injured (a).
   I removed my hat (a).
   I had a fractured skull (a).
   I found that I had a fractured skull (a).
7. A car came out of nowhere (a).
   The car was invisible (a).
   The car struck my vehicle (a).
   The car vanished (a).
8. I was coming home (a).
   I drove into the wrong house (a).
   I collided with a tree (a).
   I don't have that tree (a).
9. A little guy was the indirect cause of this accident (a).
   The little guy was in a car (a).
   The car was small (a).

The little guy [or the small car] had a mouth (a).

The mouth was big (a).

10. The accident happened (a).

The right front door of a car came around the corner (a).

The right front door of the car did not give a signal (a).

The right front door of a car came around the corner and did not give a signal (a).

EXERCISE C. Presupposes the second section but not the third. In each pair given below, the first is more positive, the second more negative.
1. Public servant, bureaucrat.
2. People's republic, totalitarian dictatorship.
3. The dearly departed, stiff.
4. Eating to excess, pigging out.
5. Soiled, filthy.
6. Lady of the night, whore.
7. Delirious with joy, giddy.
8. Captain of industry, robber baron.
9. United in holy matrimony, hitched.
10. Cognitively handicapped, a few bricks shy of a full load.

EXERCISE D. Presupposes the third section. This exercise is the inverse of B and F, asking students to reassemble isolated propositions into a single sentence and giving them a feel for the combinatorial power of language. One might ask students to work in groups, competing to see who can produce the sentence with the fewest words.

1. John has been practicing for the marathon, and did not find his seven-mile run yesterday very strenuous.

2. Professor Nash, an anthropologist at Ellipse University, holds that Tupperware was invented by Neanderthal man—a view not widely accepted among anthropologists.

3. Opposites are usually not attracted to each other, but Lauren, who loves opera, and George, who hates it, have been happily married for ten years.

4. If freedom of speech is a necessary component of a democracy—and it is—then a country that censors

newspapers, as Ruritania does, is not a democracy.

5. The law generally holds a manufacturer responsible for harm caused by its product, unless it warns the buyer that the product is dangerous or the buyer is harmed through his own negligence.

EXERCISE E. Presupposes the second and third sections. Where it seems debatable whether two assertions are equivalent, I have included them both.
1. Hamlet is always thinking about what he should do.
   Hamlet cannot decide what to do.
   Hamlet never acts.
2. The soul existed before birth.
   The soul is immortal.
   The soul is indestructible.
   The body dies.
   The soul and body are distinct.
3. Society may restrict the liberty of the individual only if his actions would harm others.
   Physical force is a way of restricting liberty.
   The moral coercion of public opinion is a way of restricting liberty.
   The individual is sovereign over his own mind and body.
   [The last proposition on the list may just be an alternative way to assert the contrapositive of the first.]

EXERCISE F. Presupposes the third section. This has the same format as B, but some of the examples are more difficult.
1. Man is born free (a).
   Man is everywhere in chains (a).
2. I went to Manderley again (e).
   Last night I dreamt I went to Manderley again (a).
3. Happy families are all alike (a).
   Every unhappy family is unhappy in its own way (a).
4. The poor in spirit are blessed (a).
   The kingdom of heaven belongs to the poor in spirit (a).

The poor in spirit are blessed because the
   kingdom of heaven belongs to them (a).
They that mourn are blessed (a).
They that mourn shall be comforted (a).
They that mourn are blessed because they shall
   be comforted (a).
The meek are blessed (a).
The meek shall inherit the earth (a).
The meek are blessed because they shall
   inherit the earth (a).
5. A single man [who is] in possession of a
   fortune must be in want of a wife (a).
   The previous proposition is universally
   acknowledged (a).
6. I come to bury Caesar (a).
   I do not come to praise Caesar (a).
   Caesar was ambitious (e).
   Brutus has told you that Caesar was ambitious
   (a).
   Brutus is noble (a).
   If Caesar was ambitious, it was a grievous
   fault (a).
   Caesar's ambition was a grievous fault (e).
   If Caesar was ambitious, he has grievously
   answered his fault (a).
   Caesar has grievously answered his fault (e).
7. The bourgeoisie has fashioned the weapons that
   bring death to itself (a).
   The bourgeoisie has called into existence the
   proletarians (a).
   The proletarians are to wield those weapons
   (a).
8. Men fear death (a).
   Children fear to go in the dark (a).
   Children's fear is increased by tales (a).
   Men's fear is increased by tales (a).
9. I went to the woods (a).
   I wished to live deliberately (a).
   I wished to front only the essential facts of
   life (a).
   I wished to see whether I could learn what
   life had to teach (a).
   I went to the woods because of those three
   wishes (a).

10. All men are created equal (a).
    All men are endowed with certain inalienable
      rights (a).
    They are so endowed by their Creator (a).
    All men have a right to life (a).
    All men have a right to liberty (a).
    All men have a right to the pursuit of
      happiness (a).
    Governments are instituted to secure these
      rights (a).
    Governments derive their powers from the
      consent of the governed (a).

EXERCISE G. Presupposes the second section. I would
ask students here to identify "loaded" language that
might bias a response. (1) and (3) plant the idea of
corporate greed and thus may encourage the answer that
the shortage is not real. The phrasing of (2), which
would be my choice as most neutral, also may encourage
that response (Can things really be as bad as all
that?!). A supplementary exercise would be to have
students look for newspaper stories that give the
exact wording of a poll question (usually near the
bottom of the story), and consider whether the
question throws any doubt on the reliability of the
results reported in the headline.

EXERCISE H. Presupposes the third section. This is a
natural lead-in to the topic of argument analysis. One
might go further with it by asking what sort of
arguments would be necessary to support each
proposition.
    Y misrepresented existing fact.
    Y intended that X rely on the misrepresentation.
    X did rely on the misrepresentation.
    X was justified in relying on it.
    X was harmed by relying on it.
As a further integrative exercise, one might evaluate
this definition by the rules of Chapter 3.

CHAPTER 5

BASIC ARGUMENT ANALYSIS

Contents

Reasoning: reasoning as a method of ascertaining the truth or falsity of propositions; the argument as a unit of reasoning; premises and conclusions; indicator words for recognizing arguments.

Diagramming Arguments: introduction of a standard technique for diagrams; additive vs. independent premises; arguments in more than one step; guidelines on using the technique.

Evaluating Arguments: distinction between truth of premises and strength of argument; strength as a matter of degree of support between premises and conclusion; the strength of an argument as a function of the strength of its component steps; implicit premises and their role in assessing strength (the "filler test").

Comments

To apply the diagramming technique to arguments in ordinary language, it is crucial to isolate the propositions that play a role, and disregard asides, disclaimers, rhetorical devices, etc. The text covers only a few of the relevant issues, since I think the problem is best dealt with through class discussion of particular examples. I would suggest spending some time on this, especially if one has not done Chapter 4.

I do not distinguish in the text between two criteria for whether premises are additive: 1) premises are additive if neither would provide any support without the other; and 2) premises are additive if the support they provide in conjunction is more than the sum of the support they would provide separately. I felt this was too subtle a distinction for students at this stage, especially since intuitive judgments about degree of support are so imprecise. Those who disagree can easily draw the distinction in class. The difference between the criteria, of course, means that some of my diagrams are subject to debate.

Many students find it hard to assess logical strength until they have studied the principles governing the specific types of argument--rules of deductive validity and inductive support. If one is not going to cover that material (Parts III and IV), I would suggest spending considerable time helping them discriminate different degrees of strength. One method is to take arguments from the text or the exercises, and ask them to think of weaker and stronger arguments having the same conclusion (in effect creating additional examples of Exercise A).

The filler test for assessing strength--find the implicit premise that would make the argument reasonably strong, and consider the plausibility of that premise--is controversial. Some people think one needs a concept of deductive validity in order to have any sense of the logical gap to be filled. Those who hold this view can easily omit this portion of the text (the final subsection of the third section). On the other hand, if one wants to cover implicit premises, but is not going to use Chapter 7, I would suggest having the students read the first section of that chapter at this point in the course.

EXERCISE A. Presupposes the third section. Each example raises possible topics for discussion. E.g., the dangers of generalizing from a single example (1), guilt by association (4). (3) is a test case for distinguishing logical strength from truth of premises.
   1. (b)
   2. (a)
   3. (b)
   4. (b)
   5. (b)

EXERCISE B. Presupposes the second section. The arguments here are simple in structure, and the diagramming easy; the emphasis is on providing further arguments to support a premise (examples are given in brackets). The point is to encourage a view of arguments as things that can be improved, expanded, deepened, not as static self-contained entities.

1. 1) If you want to see deer in the woods, you have to be quiet
   2) Deer tend to run when they hear noise

[Deer are timid animals]

2. 1) Gas is highly flammable
   2) A gallon of gas has enough explosive power to propel two tons of metal for twenty miles or more
   3) It is extremely dangerous to carry a can of gasoline in the trunk of your car

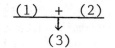

[In support of (2): A two-ton car may get 20+ mpg]

3. (1) We should not give in to the demands of terrorists when they take hostages
   (2) Giving in will convince them that their tactic works
   (3) If they are convinced that their tactic works, they will use it again

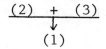

[In support of (3): People tend to rely on means they have used successfully in the past to achieve their ends]

4. (1) There is a significant difference between totalitarian governments on the left and authoritarian governments on the right
   (2) Authoritarian governments sometimes give way to democratic ones
   (3) Totalitarian governments never give way to democratic ones

$$\frac{(2) \quad + \quad (3)}{(1)}$$

[In support of (2): specific examples such as the Philippines]

5. (1) Religious cults typically demand that followers regard the leader's life as more valuable, and his judgment more reliable, than their own
   (2) Self-confident peole would not find either demand acceptable
   (3) Few self-confident people are attracted to cults

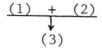

$$\frac{(1) \quad + \quad (2)}{(3)}$$

[In support of (2): Self-confident people tend to trust their own judgment and value their own lives]

EXERCISE C. Presupposes the second section. If one has done the third section, one might get more mileage out of this exercise by asking students to assess the strength of the argument prior to diagramming it, then reassess it after diagramming. I have not filled in any implicit premises here, but one might want to do so.

1. 1) No side of a man's life is unimportant to society.
   2) Whatever a man is, does, or thinks affects his well-being.
   3) A man's well-being is a matter of common concern.
   4) Whatever a man is, does, or thinks may affect those with whom he comes in contact.

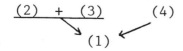

2. Not an argument, but a set of prescriptions

3. 1) There are biological dispositions toward crime
   2) Circumstances that activate criminal behavior in one person will not do so in another
   3) Social forces cannot deter crime in 100 percent of a population
   4) Distributions of crime within and across societies may, to some extent, reflect underlying distributions of constitutional factors

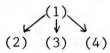

4. 1) All psychotherapies work to some extent
   2) The nonplacebo therapies propose different explanations of their effects
   3) The nonplacebos probably work by means other than the ones specified in their accompanying theories

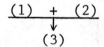

5. Not an argument

6. 1) The Soviet Union is not a great commercial power
   2) Its only products Americans would want to buy are certain raw materials
   3) Oil and gas are the main raw materials it exports
   4) It is having production problems in oil and gas
   5) It is faced with falling world market prices for oil and gas

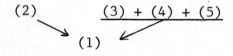

One might argue that (2) does not provide an independent argument, and should be combined additively with the other premises.

7. 1) To a plant, breathing involves a built-in cost-benefit analysis
   2) The wider the gas-exchanging pores on the leaf surface are open, the greater the supply of carbon dioxide for photosynthesis
   3) Wide-open pores allow evaporation of water
   4) The plant must balance the benefits of increased carbon dioxide against the cost of water loss

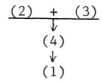

One could argue that (1) is a metaphorical restatement of (4), and thus not a distinct conclusion.

8. 1) The Rolling Stones' lives embodied evil
   2) Evil is the inability to acknowledge the suffering of others
   3) The Stones left lives destroyed in their wake
   4) The Stones were indifferent to this destruction
   5) They bore and forgot illegitimate children
   6) Their friends got hooked on drugs
   7) Some of those friends died

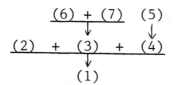

9. Not an argument

10. 1) The newly discovered poem is not by Shakespeare
    2) It is unlike any poem (known to have been) written by Shakespeare
    3) We know from early poems what Shakespeare's style was like
    4) Shakespeare was famous in his own time
    5) People at that time published poems under his name that were not his

6) People at that time would not have overlooked
   any genuine poem of his
7) The newly discovered poem is ordinary

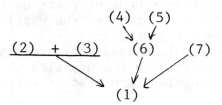

The logical relations among (4), (5), and (6)--and the
intended role of (7)--are far from clear in the text.

11. 1) A stock is worth all the cash it will return to
       investors in the future, discounted by an
       interest rate
    2) When interest rates fall, investors put higher
       values on future corporate earnings and
       dividends
    3) When interest rates fall, investors bid up
       share prices
    4) Lower interest rates mean lower yields on
       investments other than stocks
    5) A fall in interest rates will stimulate the
       stock market

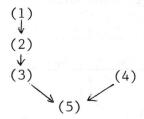

If (3) and (5) assert the same proposition, a
plausible reading, then the lower left-hand arrow
should go from (2) to (5) directly.

12. 1) Evolution rewards individuals most successful
       in passing their genes to surviving generations
    2) In sexual procreation, a female dilutes her
       genes with those of a male
    3) Sexual procreation is evolutionarily
       inefficient (in that respect)

4) Most species have retained sexual procreation
5) Sexual procreation must provide advantages sufficient to outweigh its inefficiency

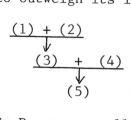

EXERCISES D and E. Presuppose all three sections, though students could do some version of either exercise at any point in the chapter. Both could be done by students working in small groups, though this might diminish somewhat the value of D, the point of which is to get students to detach judgments of logical strength from their individual opinions regarding the conclusion.

CHAPTER 6

FALLACIES

Contents

Comments

The chapter makes use of the diagramming technique from Chapter 5, but only in simple forms that could easily be explained if one is not doing that chapter.

Various fallacies are mentioned in passing in later chapters, but this should not cause problems if one skips this chapter.

I mention the classical description of these fallacies as fallacies of relevance, but I don't stress it. The term "relevance" doesn't seem to convey anything distinctive about these fallacies, and the premise of a question-begging argument is not logically irrelevant to the conclusion (though it is epistemologically irrelevant). I suggest that students treat these as an initial list of fallacies to which they should add as they encounter new ones (e.g., hasty generalization) later on.

Subjectivism is not on any traditional list of fallacies. I include it for two reasons. It helps students see what's wrong with appeal to majority and appeal to emotion. And many students accept a facile type of relativism that makes them resist the very idea of a fallacy; I find it helpful to discuss this frankly at the outset.

The classification of fallacies implied by the division into sections won't carry much weight. Some division was necessary for the sake of organization, and I think this is a natural grouping of the particular fallacies I wanted to include. But I

wouldn't put much stress on it, or go out of my way to
assimilate other fallacies to it. That's one reason I
included Exercise D.

All of the exercises presuppose all three
sections of the text.

EXERCISE A
1. Appeal to majority
2. Subjectivism
3. Appeal to authority or force, depending on
intent
4. Circular reasoning [not appeal to majority]
5. Appeal to ignorancce
6. Diversion
7. Begging the question or ad hominem
8. Ad hominem/tu quoque
9. Complex question
10. Appeal to majority

EXERCISE B. Having to create examples of specific
fallacies is a good way to learn the differences among
them. An extension would be to have students make up
fallacies from scratch, in the format of Exercise A.
1. Either ghosts exist or Mary lied...
2. The popularity of entrepreneurs implies...
3. Tom Jones' stomach cancer disappeared when...
4. Doctor Spock says...
5. Whaling is a good metaphor for the human
condition...
6. Uncle Sam wants your money!
7. It has never been proved that crimes are not
caused by TV violence.
8. Because logic has a lot of value and deserves
your attention...
9. I can't bear to think of failing...
10. Capitalism squeezes out all the creative
energy of workers into products sold for obscene
profits, returning only a trickle to the workers...

EXERCISE C
1. Appeal to majority
2. Post hoc
3. Non sequitur
4. Appeal to majority

5. Ad hominem/poisoning the well, possibly appeal to emotion
6. Appeal to force
7. Appeal to authority, appeal to majority [the first point ("undermines the basic premise") might be begging the question]
8. Appeal to emotion [the phrase "the direct killing..." might be construed as a nonemotive argument, but then one should consider whether it begs the question]
9. Post hoc [if one is not going to cover Chapter 12, this might be an occasion for discussing what proof of causality would require in this case]
10. Appeal to ignorance; possibly non sequitur
11. Begging the question
12. Ad hominem
13. Subjectivism
14. Post hoc
15. Appeal to majority
16. Appeal to ignorance
17. Straw man
18. Begging the question
19. Ad hominem

EXERCISE D. This is an integrative exercise, presupposing Chapter 2. To get discussion going, it might be useful to show students how other textbooks classify the fallacies. Questions to consider:

Could any fallacies from the first two sections be equally well considered fallacies of logical structure?

Appeal to majority and appeal to authority are quite similar; should they be classified together?

Should appeal to force be considered a fallacy at all, or is it outside the realm of argument, even bad argument, altogether?

EXERCISE E. Another integrative exercise, presupposing Chapter 5. In addition to requiring the use of diagrams, it encourages students to integrate what they've learned about fallacies with the general concept of logical strength. It is not clear how to diagram some of these arguments; I would suggest to students that such difficulty may be the fault of the

argument, a mark of unclarity, and not a failure on
their part.

1. 1) This Administration has been attacked for going
too far in pursuing affirmative action
2) This Administration has been attacked for not
going far enough on affirmative action
3) This Administration occupies a middle position
on affirmative action
4) This Administration's policy will help correct
discrimination

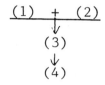

The step from (3) to (4) seems a clear <u>non sequitur</u>,
and even the first step is dubious, since (1) and (2)
don't really tell us what the range of opinion is.
One might also see an appeal to majority here, in the
assumption that one's location on the spectrum of
opinion implies something about the objective efficacy
of one's policy.

2. 1) If the task of the painter were to copy for men
what they see, the critic could make only a
single judgment: that the copy is right or wrong
2) The critic is not limited to a single judgment
3) The task of the painter is not to copy for men
what they see

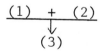

The rhetorical device in the formulation of (2)--"No
one who has read a page"--might be regarded as an
appeal to majority or to authority (the elite of the
well educated). If one is not going to use the
chapters on deduction, it might be worth isolating the
<u>modus tollens</u> structure of the argument.

3. 1) Americans should not own handguns
   2) Selling firearms is big business
   3) Those opposed to selling firearms have to battle powerful lobbies
   4) The lobbies fight to keep profits for the arms manufacturers

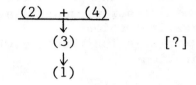

Could be <u>non sequitur</u>, or appeal to emotion (sympathy for those who have to battle against odds).

4. 1) Certain chemicals cause cancer in humans
   2) Certain chemicals cause cancer in animals
   3) All chemicals known to induce cancer in humans cause cancer in animals
   4) Reducing exposure to chemicals known or suspected to cause cancer in humans or animals will reduce chemically induced cancer in humans

$$\frac{(1) \; + \; (2) \; + \; (3)}{(4)} \qquad [?]$$

One could unpack the conclusion here: 4a) reducing exposure to chemicals known to cause cancer in <u>humans</u> will reduce chemically induced cancer in humans; 4b) reducing exposure to chemicals known to induce cancer in <u>animals</u> will reduce chemically induced cancer in humans. (4a) is very nearly a tautology, depending at most on (1). The inference from (3) to (4b) is a <u>non sequitur</u>; what (4b) requires is the converse of (3). This might be an occasion for discussing the logic of categorical propositions, especially if one is not going to cover Chapter 8.

5. 1) Braniff set off on a course of [irresponsible, mindless] cost-is-no-object expansion
   2) Braniff had accumulated a debt of $288 million in its first 30 years
   3) In the three years following deregulation, it borrowed $451 million to finance expansion

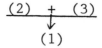

$$\frac{(2)\ +\ (3)}{(1)}$$

The bracketed terms in (1) are suggestions for interpreting the metaphorical phrases. One's interpretation will affect the degree of evidence necessary to support this conclusion. (2) and (3) may provide some evidence, but in the absence of evidence regarding profit expectations, the behavior of other airlines, etc., the argument may be a <u>non sequitur</u>.

6. 1) The majority of the States have had restrictions on abortions for at least a century
   2) The restrictions reflect majority sentiment within the States that have them
   3) The right to an abortion is not so deeply rooted in the traditions and conscience of our people as to be ranked fundamental

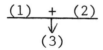

$$\frac{(1)\ +\ (2)}{(3)}$$

This looks like appeal to majority, but if the conclusion is interpreted as a statement about majority sentiment, then evidence about majority sentiment is relevant to it.

7. 1) One cannot prove that something does not exist
   2) There is always a chance that it does exist but no one has seen it
   3) One cannot prove that something does not cause cancer
   4) There is always the chance that it does cause cancer but it hasn't shown up yet

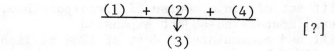

$$\frac{(1) + (2) + (4)}{\downarrow} \quad [?]$$
$$(3)$$

The obvious topic for discussion here is whether this
is an appeal to ignorance, or a valid point about
scientific methodology.

ADVANCED ARGUMENT ANALYSIS

Contents

Assumed Premises: guidelines for selecting an implicit premise; the principle of charity.

Distilling an Argument: extracting an argument from a longer passage.

Diagramming Debates: types of incompatible conclusions; diagramming counterarguments; an extended example.

Comments

This chapter is intended primarily for those who want to devote considerable time to the general method of argument analysis. If one is going to cover Parts III and IV in any depth, this chapter will probably have to be omitted, though in that case I would recommend using the first section, and perhaps some of the exercises (e.g., B), to supplement Chapter 5.

The chapter presupposes Chapter 5 but not Chapter 6. Each of the three sections within the chapter is independent.

In addition to the specific presuppositions cited for each exercise, all of them presuppose Chapter 5.

EXERCISE A. Presupposes the first section.

1. A judge should not have an interest that biases his judgment.

2. Knowledge is an end in itself.

3. a) Anything written for the masses is somewhat trite and conventional. b) Trite and conventional information will not make you rich.

4. a) A language has a deep structure distinct from its surface structure. b) The deep structure is dependent on [determined by?] the brain.

5. America's domestic drug consumption contributes to its drug problems.

EXERCISE B. Presupposes the first two sections.

1. 1) The government is an agent of the people
   a) An agent who keeps secrets from its principal
      betrays the trust of its principal
   2) An attorney who kept secrets from his client
      would betray the client's trust
   b) An attorney is an agent for his client
   c) It is wrong to betray a trust
   3) The government should not keep secrets from the
      people

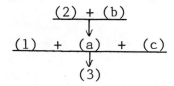

This is an argument by analogy, dependent on the
strength of the similarity between a private attorney
and the government. On my view (see Chapter 13), the
argument involves an implicit inference from the
case of the attorney to a generalization about agents
(a), a weak generalization from a single example.

2. 1) A tree develops vertically only at the top
   2) The points where the branches spring from the
      trunk stay at the same level
   3) A wire fence nailed to the trunk does not rise
      as the tree grows
   4) A wire fence nailed to the trunk stays at the
      same level as the fence nailed to posts

This seems fairly strong.

3. 1) Crotonaldehyde may not be the ingredient that
      causes some people to break out in hives when
      they eat strawberries
   2) Raspberries contain crotonaldehyde

3) Some people who get hives from eating
   strawberries do not get hives from eating
   raspberries
a) The levels of crotonaldehyde in raspberries and
   strawberries are comparable

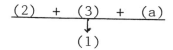

$$\frac{(2) \ + \ (3) \ + \ (a)}{(1)}$$

This seems fairly strong, especially given the
tentative nature of the conclusion. If one is not
going to cover Mill's methods (Chapter 12), this might
be an occasion to discuss varying the factors to
establish causal connections.

4. 1) Insurance companies do not face any significant
      risk from insuring day care centers
   2) Insurance journals have not run any articles
      describing day care as "high risk" or "high
      loss"
   a) If insuring day care centers involved high risk
      or high loss, insurance journals would have said
      so
   3) Liability claims involving child care and pre-
      school are rare
   4) Settlements from these (rare) claims were not
      large
   5) Numerous agents and brokers agree with (3) and
      (4)
   6) No jury has made an award for a case of abuse at
      a day care center
   b) Abuse would be the only significant basis for a
      liability claim against a day care center

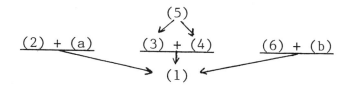

The right-hand argument seems weaker than the other
two, since the implicit premise (b) is questionable—
what about claims arising from accidental injuries? In
the middle argument, the reference to expert judgment

is legitimate in principle; but we don't know how many experts were consulted, or how diligently the author looked for experts who disagreed.

5. 1) All physical bodies are a mixture of matter and empty space
   2) Rocky cave roofs exude moisture
   3) Sweat, hair, and food pass through our bodies
   4) Voices, scent, heat, and cold pass through stone and iron
   a) All physical bodies allow other things to pass through them
   b) A thing that allows other things to pass through it has empty spaces

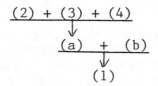

There are other ways to diagram this argument. I've done it this way to separate the element of inductive generalization--the inference to (a)--and the implicit premise (b) that governs the explanatory conclusion. It is possible to treat (2), (3), and (4) as nonadditive instead of additive premises, depending on one's view of induction.

6. 1) Confiscating books is not a violation of freedom of speech
   2) Confiscating books is the highest affirmation of freedom of speech
   3) Freedom to propagandize fascism is the kind of freedom that all honest people oppose
   a) The confiscated books propagandize fascism
   b) Freedom that honest people oppose is not part of freedom of speech
   4) The confiscated books stir up hatred and hostility among people
   c) Books that stir up hatred and hostility are not protected by freedom of speech
   5) The confiscated books hamper the process of detente

d) Books that hamper detente are not protected by
   freedom of speech

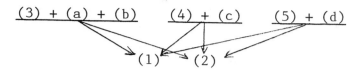

$$\underline{(3) + (a) + (b)} \quad \underline{(4) + (c)} \quad \underline{(5) + (d)}$$
$$(1) \quad (2)$$

This is an example of the way a weaseling bit of
propaganda can be analyzed by the same method as more
appealing arguments, allowing one to identify specific
objections. I have treated (1) and (2) as separate
propositions, but one might also regard (2) as a
rhetorical exaggeration of (1), so that there is only
one conclusion. Assessment of strength will depend on
the implicit premises.

7. 1) SATs serve a valid function
   2) The SAT is a standardized, nation-wide test
   3) Such tests allow colleges to recruit from all
      over the country
   4) Nation-wide recruitment allows colleges to get
      academically elite students
   a) Challenging the academic elite is a preferable
      function for colleges to grooming the socially
      elite

$$\underline{(2) \ + \ (3) \ + \ (4) \ + \ (a)}$$
$$(1)$$

This is intended as an example of the way very good
writing can hide logical holes. "Challenging the
academic elite" is a pretty vague description of what
SATs allow colleges to do. It is given content by
contrast with "grooming the socially elite," but this
is gratuitous. At most the premises tell us that
without SATs colleges would be limited to challenging
the local, instead of the nation-wide, academically
elite.

EXERCISE C. Presupposes the third section. The
examples include a violation of a canon of inductive
reasoning (2), and a deductively invalid argument (3).
One might use this exercise to introduce these topics

and/or contrast inductive and deductive reasoning.

1. 1) Antitrust laws promote competition
   a) Competition is essential to free enterprise
   2) Antitrust laws help maintain the free enterprise
      system
   3) Large firms have a tendency to acquire monopoly
      power
   4) Large firms have a tendency to drive out smaller
      firms
   5) Antitrust laws counteract these tendencies

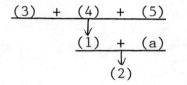

One could challenge premises (3), (4), or (5) on
economic grounds. One could challenge the strength of
the inference to (1) by attacking the assumption that
antitrust laws have no significant anti-competitive
effects.

2. 1) Scotch and soda made me drunk
   2) Brandy and soda made me drunk
   3) Wine and soda made me drunk
   4) Soda causes inebriation

$$\frac{(1) + (2) + (3)}{(4)}$$

The strength of the inference rests on the assumption
that soda is the only common factor. If one is not
going to cover Chapter 12, this could be the occasion
for comment on inductive methods of establishing
causal connections.

3. 1) Anyone who has self-esteem wants to be loved for
      himself
   a) No one who wants to be loved for himself wants
      unconditional love
   2) No one who has self-esteem wants unconditional
      love

3) Anyone who lacks self-esteem wants unconditional
   love

The example is written so that students, hopefully,
will sense that (3) does not follow from (2). One can
then show that the implicit premise necessary to fill
the gap would be a false abstract statement pertaining
to the logical form of the argument, e.g., If no S is
P, then all non-S are P. This could serve as a preview
for the syllogism. If one is not going to cover the
syllogism, I would suggest skipping this example.

4. 1) The supply of housing has increased rapidly
   2) The generation born in the 1960s and 1970s is
      relatively small
   3) When this generation enters the housing market,
      demand will fall
   4) Increased supply will then face decreased
      demand
   a) When the supply of a good increases and demand
      falls, the price falls
   5) Housing prices will fall
   b) If housing prices fall, the construction
      industry will suffer
   6) The construction industry will suffer

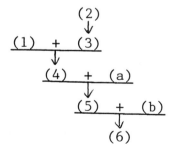

This is a chain of predictions whose premises are hard
to challenge, but whose strength depends on implicit
ceteris paribus clauses that might be challenged--

e.g., that government policy will not change in a way that affects prices, or that native births (not immigration) are the major determinant of population levels, etc.

EXERCISE D. Presupposes the first section, and Chapter 3. This is an integrative exercise; the purpose is to review the material on definitions, and to see how definitions play a role in arguments. I have omitted the diagrams below, and stated only the definitional premises.

1. News is what protrudes from the ordinary. Metaphorical. If the metaphor is cashed in terms of the concept of significant or unusual events, the question is whether the argument supports the view that in a nation such as ours, such events will be predominantly negative rather than positive.

2. A commentator is an unfair [non-objective?] writer. Even if one accepts the description of commentators as unfair or nonobjective, so that the definition is not too narrow, this would surely be on the grounds that they express their opinions, so that the definition is nonessential.

3. The argument seems to assume that for the purposes of taxation, money one contributes to philanthropy should not count as income. This suggests a definition of income as money received and spent on oneself. The point for discussion is whether this is too narrow.

4. A desirable thing is something people desire. By the ordinary concept of the desirable as something worthy of being desired, this is too broad and too narrow.

EXERCISE E. Presupposes the third section. This is intended as a comic interlude, especially if one arranges to play the song in class. I have exercised a degree of poetic license in my analysis below.

A1) You are a success now
A2) You were a cocktail waitress when I met you
Aa) Without me you would still be a cocktail waitress
A3) You owe your success to me
A4) I can put you back down
A5) You still need me

A6) You should stay with me

B1) I would have succeeded without you
B2) I need independence

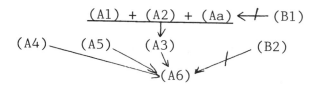

(A4) sounds like an appeal to force, especially given
the last line of the male part. (B2) is stated in a
way that suggests subjectivism.

EXERCISE F. Presupposes the third section. If one is
doing this in class discussion, I would start by
getting agreement on the best diagram of the debate in
the Practice Quiz, either the one I give in the
Answers section or some alternative. Students can then
use the diagram to organize a search for further
points to make on each side.

EXERCISE G. Presupposes the third section.

A1) Air bags in cars should not be required
A2) In front-end collisions, they function no better
    than seat belts
A3) In side and rear crashes they are useless
Aa) They do not increase safety
A4) They create a hazard by accidental deployment
A5) They cost nearly $200
Ab) $200 is a lot of money
Ac) They are expensive
A6) Consumers have shown little interest in them
A7) GM succeeded in selling only 6,000

B1) Airbags function well
B2) GM admits they work well in tests and on highways
B3) They have saved lives
B4) They have the potential to save 10,000 lives and a
million injuries annually
B5) They become visible only in a crash
B6) They cost less than a vinyl roof

B7) The money they save in lower insurance costs and lower crash-imposed costs is greater than their price
B8) Former GM President Ed Cole has them in his car
B9) DeLorean, AllState and Forbes favor requiring them by law
B10) Requiring them by law would be compassionate

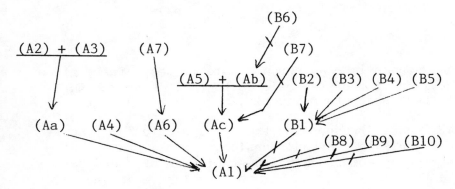

Comments: The factual claims used to attack and support (Aa) and (B1) conflict, and can't be resolved on the basis of information contained within the argument. The authors argue about the advantages and disadvantages of air bags, whereas the conclusion concerns a government action; neither cites a principle connecting the two issues (though (A6) suggests that Bleiberg thinks consumers should be free to choose, and (B7) suggests that Nader thinks anything affecting government expenditures should be subject to regulation). (B8) and (B9) may be appeals to authority, and (B10) an appeal to emotion (pity).

EXERCISE H. Presupposes the third section. If this is done in class, students could work in pairs, or pairs of groups, with one student or group responsible for the A side of the debate, the other for the B side.

CHAPTER 8

CATEGORICAL PROPOSITIONS

Contents

Standard Form: subject and predicate terms, quality and quantity; some rules for translating into standard form.

The Square of Opposition: contraries, contradictories, subalternates, and subcontraries.

Distribution: standard rules for subject and predicate terms.

Immediate Inference: converse, obverse, and contrapositive.

Comments

I have tried to keep the material in this chapter to the minimum required for understanding the categorical syllogism. I included the final section, on immediate inferences, because conversion helps students understand exactly what is (and is not) asserted by categorical propositions, and because obversion is useful in translating arguments into standard categorical form. But the section does add a lot to the memory load. It can be omitted, but a few references in Chapter 9 will have to be explained.

Throughout this chapter and the next, I have proceeded on the classical assumption that universal categorical propositions have existential import. This reflects my view that in ordinary language and reasoning, the distinction between statements that have and statements that lack existential import is a matter of context and conversational implicature, and does not coincide with the particular-universal distinction. Those who want to cover this material on the opposite assumption should probably skip the second section and present the alternative square of opposition in class.

Some instructors may want to introduce the Venn representations of categorical propositions in connection with this chapter. I have not done so because the modification necessary to handle the

existential import of universal propositions makes
them rather cumbersome (see comments, Chapter 9), and
because the A proposition and its contrapositive do
not come out as equivalent with this modification. I
find the modified diagrams are useful only as a
calculation device for syllogistic validity.

EXERCISE A. Presupposes the first and third sections.
Translating from standard into nonstandard form is
easier than, and gives students an initial feel for,
translating from nonstandard into standard form.
    1. O. S: undistributed, P: distributed.
    2. E. S and P both distributed.
    3. A. S: distributed, P: undistributed.
    4. E: S and P both distributed.
    5. I. S and P both undistributed.
    6. A. S: distributed, P: undistributed.
    7. I. S and P both distributed.
    8. O. S: undistributed, P: distributed.
    9. I. S and P both undistributed.
  10. E. S and P both distributed.

EXERCISE B. Presupposes all four sections. I have not
translated all the predicates into class terms.
    1. All sonnets have fourteen lines. A. S:
distributed, P: undistributed. [No sonnet has fourteen
lines.]
    2. Some metals are things that rust. I. S and P
both undistributed. [Some things that rust are
metals.]
    3. Some fish are not carnivores. O. S:
undistributed, P: distributed. [Some fish are non-
carnivores.]
    4. No human being is a person who has run the
mile in less than 3:40. E. S and P both distributed.
[Some human being is a person who has run the mile in
less than 3:40.]
    5. All countries with the word "Democratic" in
their official name are communist dictatorships. A. S:
distributed, P: undistributed. [All countries that are
not communist dictatorships are countries that do not
have the word "Democratic" in their official name.]

6. That man in the corner is drunk. A. S: distributed, P: undistributed. [That man in the corner is not non-drunk.]

7. No big girl is a person who cries. E. S and P both distributed. [All big girls cry.]

8. All war is hell (a hellish thing). A. S: distributed, P: undistributed. [Some war is not hell.]

9. Some person is knocking at my door. I. S and P both distributed. [Some person is not knocking at my door.]

10. All sugar is sweet. A. S: distributed, P: undistributed. [Some sugar is sweet.]

11. You are sweet. A. S: distributed, P: undistributed. [You are not unsweet.]

12. Some men are at work. I. S and P both undistributed. [No men are at work.]

13. Some deer were at the edge of the clearing. I. S and P both undistributed. [Some deer were not at the edge of the clearing.]

14. Some criminals are not people from poor families. O. S: undistributed, P: distributed. [Some people from non-poor families are not non-criminals.]

15. Alice is not a person who lives here. E. S and P both distributed. [Alice is a person who lives here.]

16. No real man is a person who eats quiche. E. S and P both distributed. [No person who eats quiche is a real man.]

17. All students who return after midnight are people required to sign in. A. S: distributed, P: undistributed. [Some people required to sign in are students who return after midnight.]

18. No law that forces a person to act against his judgment is a just law. E. S and P both distributed. [No law that does not force a person to act against his judgment is an unjust law.]

19. Some proposals put forward for the control of nuclear arms are not proposals that would affect the levels of submarine-based missiles. O. S: undistributed, P: distributed. [All proposals put forward for the control of nuclear arms are proposals that would affect the levels of submarine-based missiles.]

20. No person knows the trouble I've seen. E. S and P both distributed. [Some people know the trouble I've seen.]

EXERCISE C. Presupposes the second and fourth sections. If this exercise is done in class, I would try to get students to see intuitively why the second proposition does or does not follow, and not just go by the rules.
    1. Subalternate. Follows.
    2. Obverse. Follows.
    3. Converse. Does not follow.
    4. Subcontrary. Does not follow.
    5. Obverse. Follows.
    6. Contrapositive. Follows.
    7. Converse. Follows.
    8. Converse by limitation. Follows.
    9. Contrapositive. Does not follow.
    10. Converse. Does not follow.

EXERCISE D. This is an integrative exercise, presupposing Chapter 4 as well as the first section of this chapter.
    1. All bad events have some good aspect.
    2. All people tend to associate with others who share the same interests (values, personalities).
    3. No great work is accomplished quickly.
    4. No one who is highly sensitive to criticism should criticize others.
    5. All money one has saved is money one has earned.
    6. All people who do not live a settled life escape the ill effects of a settled life. [I have translated this one into the vaguest possible terms, turning it into a tautology. I would challenge students to come up with a more substantive literal claim.]
    7. All persons with advance warning of a threat are people who can prepare for it.
    8. All people who possess great power are people fearful of and vigilant toward those who would dispossess them.
    9. All suggestions or requests backed by financial inducements have a good chance of succeeding. [I think this is truer to the proverb than

the broader alternative "All wealthy people are powerful," but this may be idiosyncratic.]

10. No valuable end is achieved without risk.

EXERCISE E. Presupposes the second and fourth sections. I have taken a certain license in some of the translations below.

1. No knowledge in his possession is useless
↓
All knowledge in his possession is useful

Obverse. Follows.

2. All nonessential federal workers went home
↓
All who did not go home are essential federal workers

Contrapositive. Follows.

3. No state that is not well armed has good laws
↓
All states that are well armed have good laws

Does not follow. To identify the problem here, one needs to lay out a series of steps necessary to get from the first proposition to the second. E.g.: take the obverse, then the contrapositive; it is then necessary to take the converse of an A proposition, an illicit step.

4. All music is feeling
↓
All feeling is music

Converse. Does not follow. [An alternative is to treat this as a syllogism: All music is feeling; my desire is a feeling; my desire is music.]

CHAPTER 9

CATEGORICAL SYLLOGISMS

Contents

The Structure of a Syllogism: major, minor, and middle terms; mood and figure.
Validity: four rules for determining validity; using obversion to eliminate a fourth (complementary) term.
Venn Diagrams: a modification of the standard diagrams to handle existential import of universal propositions.
Enthymemes: using rules of validity to find an assumed premise.

Comments

I include a brief discussion of mood and figure in the first section because I have found this to be the most economical way to give students a grasp of the structure of the syllogism, and because I believe the differences among the figures have some psychological reality for reasoning. But none of the rules for validity depend on this material.

To be used under the existential interpretation of universal propositions, Venn diagrams must include x's in the universal as well as particular propositions. This makes them more cumbersome, especially since two x's must be used for the E proposition. To simplify a bit, one could tell students that if the conclusion is universal, they can omit the x̄'s for all the universal propositions, and the method will still work.

EXERCISE A. Presupposes the second section and/or the third.
   1. Valid.
   2. Invalid: two negative premises.
   3. Invalid: two negative premises.
   4. Invalid: illicit major.
   5. Valid.

6. Valid.
7. Invalid: illicit major.
8. Invalid: neg. premise, affirm. conclusion.
9. Invalid: undistributed middle.
10. Invalid: undistributed middle.
11. Invalid: illicit minor.
12. Invalid: illicit major.
13. Valid.
14. Valid.
15. Invalid: undistributed middle.

EXERCISE B. Presupposes the first three sections.

1. All states that ignore human rights are tyrannies
   Some democracies are states that ignore human
        rights
   Some democracies are tyrannies
AII-1. Valid

2. All students who cram for a test do poorly on it
   Amy did poorly on the test
   Amy crammed for the test
AAA-2. Invalid: undistributed middle

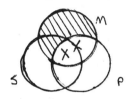

3. No plant is capable of locomotion
   All amoebas are capable of locomotion
   No amoeba is a plant
EAE-2. Valid

4. All who supported the Voting Rights Bill oppose
        racial discrimination
   No conservative supported the Voting Rights Bill
   No conservative opposes racial discrimination
AEE-1. Invalid: illicit major

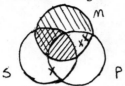

5. All noise is a disorderly progression of sounds
   No music is a disorderly progression of sounds
   No music is noise
AEE-2. Valid

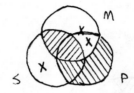

6. No course in which the grade is based exclusively
        on essays is graded objectively
   Some courses in which the grade is based
        exclusively on essays are not philosophy
        courses
   Some philosophy courses are graded objectively
EOI-3. Invalid: two neg. premises, affirm. conclusion

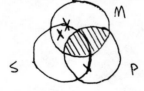

7. All people who overreact to the charge of envy are
        envious
   No person with a strong sense of justice is
        envious
   No person with a strong sense of justice overreacts
        to the charge of envy
AEE-2. Valid

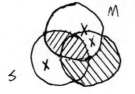

-58-

8. No nonprofit organization sells stock
   Some hospital corporations sell stock
   Some hospital corporations are not nonprofit
         corporations
EIO-2. Valid

9. Some international conflicts arise from honest
         motives
   No aggressive war arises from honest motives
   Some aggressive wars are not international
         conflicts
IEO-2. Invalid: illicit major

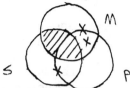

10. Some people who depend on reputation are
         dishonest
    All politicians depend on reputation
    Some politicians are dishonest
IAI-1. Invalid: undistributed middle

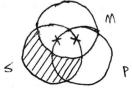

11. No great orchestra conductor is careless
    Some great orchestra conductors are flamboyant
    Some flamboyant people are not careless
EIO-3. Valid

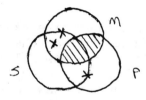

EXERCISE C. Presupposes the first section, though the
second would help. This is a creative exercise;
students might be asked to work in groups, perhaps
with competition for the most plausible (humorous,
unexpected) syllogisms. My examples below are mere
suggestions.

1. No Civil War movie ever made a nickel
   Gone With the Wind is a Civil War movie
   Gone With the Wind will not make a nickel

2. Anything that is undeservedly forgotten is a good
           topic for a doctoral thesis
   Some books are undeservedly forgotten
   Some books are good topics for doctoral theses

   All books that are remembered deserve to be
           remembered
   McGuffey's Readers are remembered
   McGuffey's Readers deserve to be remembered

3. All people who speak much are much mistaken
   No one worth listening to is much mistaken
   No one worth listening to speaks much

4. All people with vices are people whom the media
           will not allow to be elected to public
           office
   Some people with vices are not contemptible
   Some people whom the media will not allow to be
           elected to public office are not
           contemptible.

EXERCISE D. Presupposes the first section, though the
rest of the chapter will help. This is another
creative exercise; see suggestions for C. If students
are having trouble, one might get them started by
giving them a conclusion.

EXERCISE E. This is an integrative exercise,
presupposing Chapter 2 as well as the first section of
this one. The point is to see how syllogisms are a
natural tool for spelling out the implications of a
classification scheme. In the answers below, I've
given only the key premise.

1. All electrons are physical entities.
2. Some bonds are municipal bonds.
3. All trees are plants.
4. Some methods of doing research involve deception of subjects.

EXERCISE F. Presupposes the chapter as a whole.

1. All material systems are governed by the laws of
        physics
   <u>All</u> living systems are material systems
   All living systems are governed by the laws of
        physics
     AAA-1. Valid

2. (All who have no superior are sovereigns)
   <u>All</u> members of a free democracy have no superior
   All members of a free democracy are sovereigns
     AAA-1. Valid

3. All people who are crazy are people who cannot
        believe they are crazy
   <u>I am</u> a person who cannot believe I am crazy
   I am crazy
     AAA-2. Invalid: undistributed middle

4. (No one who rejoices at the expense of other men
        can expect to thrive in the world of men)
   <u>All</u> who rejoice loudly of their victories rejoice
        at the expense of other men
   No one who rejoices loudly of his victories can
        expect to thrive in the world of men
     EAE-1. Valid

5. (All people who answer every question put to them
        are tremendously ignorant)
   <u>That</u> man answers every question put to him
   That man is tremendously ignorant
     AAA-1. Valid

6. All cruel punishments are either particularly
        painful or particularly undeserved
   <u>The</u> death penalty is not either particularly
        painful or particularly undeserved
   The death penalty is not a cruel punishment
      AEE-2. Valid

7. No man of merit has a right to the grace of God
   <u>I am</u> not a man of merit
   I have a right to the grace of God
      EEA-1. Invalid: two neg. premises, affirm.
         conclusion

8. (All people who do not revert to normalcy after a
        violent episode are insane)
   <u>Some</u> individuals who suffer organic abnormalities
        or psychoses that produce rage attacks do
        not revert to normalcy after a violent
        episode
   Some individuals who suffer organic abnormalities
        or psychoses that produce rage attacks are
        insane
      AII-1. Valid

9. No person who dies from unforeseen causes has an
        agitated expression on his face
   <u>This</u> man had an agitated expression on his face
   This man did not die from unforeseen causes
      EAE-2. Valid

10. No good thing harms its owner
    <u>Some</u> wealth harms its owners
    (Some wealth is not a good thing)
       EIO-2. Valid

11. (No wealth is genetic)
    <u>Some</u> wealth runs in families
    Some things that run in families are not genetic
       EIO-3. Valid

EXERCISE G. Presupposes the square of opposition from
Chapter 8, as well as the first two sections of this
chapter. Asking students to create invalid syllogisms
has the same purpose as asking them to construct
fallacious arguments (Chapter 6, Exercise B): it helps

develop an intuitive feel for invalidity. If one does the full exercise, asking them to create valid arguments for and against each proposition, it also helps them realize the importance of the premises from which one starts.

EXERCISE H. Presupposes the first two sections. This exercise could serve as a way of strengthening students' feel for the different figures, but it is mainly intended to elicit theoretical interest in more advanced students.

1. The middle term in this figure is in the predicate of both premises. It will not be distributed, therefore, unless one premise is negative, in which case the conclusion must be negative.

2. If the minor premise is negative, the conclusion must be negative as well, which means the predicate will be distributed. This means the major term will have to be distributed in the major premise, which can happen only if the major premise is negative, giving one two negative premises.

3. If the conclusion is universal, the subject term is distributed, which would require a negative minor premise, which would require a negative conclusion whose predicate is distributed, which would require a negative major premise, giving one two negative premises.

4 and 5. These have to be done by looking at each figure in turn.

CHAPTER 10

DISJUNCTIVE AND HYPOTHETICAL SYLLOGISMS

Contents

Disjunctive Syllogisms: basic form of the syllogism, missing premises, inclusive versus exclusive "or."

Hypothetical Syllogisms: pure hypothetical syllogism; modus ponens, modus tollens, and associated invalid forms.

Nonstandard Forms: "not both p and q," "only if," "if and only if," "unless," "whenever."

Comments

This chapter could be covered before doing Chapters 8 and 9, for those who want to follow the modern rather than the classical Aristotelian order. In that case, one would need to explain the concept of validity.

For theoretical reasons, I would have preferred to introduce the concepts of necessary and sufficient conditions in connection with hypothetical propositions, rather than waiting until the discussion of causality in Chapter 12. In teaching, however, I found that this didn't help most students in understanding the relationships between antecedent and consequent. It only gave them an alternative way to describe the relationships, which they experienced as an added burden in mastering already difficult material.

EXERCISE A. Presupposes all three sections.
1. Invalid
2. Valid
3. Valid
4. Invalid
5. Invalid
6. Invalid
7. Valid
8. Valid

9. Invalid
10. Invalid
11. Invalid
12. Invalid
13. Invalid
14. Valid

EXERCISE B. Presupposes the chapter as a whole.

1. If I did not hurry, I would be late
   I hurried
   I was not late
     Denying the antecedent. Invalid

2. If I am willing to take statistics, then it is
           offered in the morning
   It is not offered in the morning
   I am not willing to take it
     Modus tollens. Valid

3. If Frank were jealous of Cindy, he would follow her
           around with a sour expression
   Frank was following her around with a sour
           expression
   Frank is jealous of Cindy
     Affirming the consequent. Invalid

4. If Mercury's period of rotation equals its period
           of revolution, then it always presents the
           same side to the Sun
   If Mercury always presents the same side to the
           Sun, then we can only see one side of it
   If Mercury's period of rotation equals its period
           of revolution, then we can only see one side
           of it
     Pure hypothetical. Valid

5. If you want milk, then there is milk in the
           refrigerator
   I don't want milk
   There is no milk in the refrigerator
     Denying the antecedent. Invalid

6. Either we negotiate with the Soviets or we make
        ourselves strong enough to resist attack
   We should make ourselves strong enough to resist
        attack
   We should not negotiate
     Affirming a disjunct. Invalid

7. If Robin is embarrassed, she gets a blotch
   Robin does not have a blotch
   Robin is not embarrassed
     Modus tollens. Valid

8. If the circuit is broken, then current will not
        flow
   The circuit is broken
   Current will not flow
     Modus ponens. Valid

9. If Rome had been cohesive enough, then it would
        have repelled the invaders
   Rome was not cohesive enough
   Rome could not repel the invaders
     Denying the antecedent. Invalid. [This is tricky
   because the statement might be taken as an
   explanation, with Rome's cohesion interpreted as a
   necessary as well as a sufficient condition for its
   capacity to resist invasion.]

10. Either I don't go to the movies or I don't study
        for the exam
    I will study for the exam
    I won't go to the movies
      Denying a disjunct. Valid

11. If you have read this far, then you are serious
        about logic
    If you are not serious about logic, then you won't
        be able to master it
    If you have read this far, then you will be able
        to master logic
      Invalid form of pure hypothetical

12. If the errors and distortions in TV news were not
        the result of political bias, then they
        would be randomly distributed across the
        political spectrum
    The errors and distortions are not randomly
        distributed
    (The errors and distortions are the result of
        political bias)
    Modus tollens. Valid

13. If men were angels, anarchy would be a fine and
        beautiful system
    Men are not angels
    (Anarchy is not a fine and beautiful system)
    Denying the antecedent. Invalid

EXERCISE C. Presupposes the first two sections.
Students are given a specific conclusion so that they
can focus their creative efforts on the logical form
requested; a further step would be to have them make
up arguments from scratch that fit these (or other)
logical forms. As in previous chapters, students are
asked to make up invalid as well as valid arguments.

EXERCISE D. Presupposes the chapter as a whole.

1. If the Moral Law was one of our instincts, then we
        ought to be able to point to a particular
        impulse that is always good
    We cannot point to a particular impulse that is
        always good
    The moral Law is not one of our instincts
        Modus tollens. Valid

2. If these charges on Watergate were true, I would
        resign
    These charges are not true
    I will not resign
        Denying the antecedent. Invalid

3. If network election projections were news reports,
        the networks would report each other's
        projections
   The networks do not report each others'
        projections
   Network projections are not news reports
     Modus tollens. Valid

4. If the White House lacks a strong and effective
        chief of staff, then it cannot function
        properly
   If the White House cannot function properly, then
        the executive branch cannot function
        effectively
   (If the White House lacks a strong and effective
        chief of staff, then the executive branch
        cannot function effectively)
     Pure hypothetical. Valid

5. If imitation is an important factor in language
        development, then it would be easy to find
        evidence of its importance
   It is not easy to find evidence of the importance
        of imitation
   Imitation is not an important factor in language
        development
     Modus tollens. Valid

6. Either Barbara Ehrenreich knows nothing about sex,
        or I know nothing about cars
   I know something about cars
   (Barbara Ehrenreich knows nothing about sex)
     Denying a disjunct. Valid

7. If the value of money should have an objective
        regulator, then it should be linked to a
        real commodity
   The value of money should have an objective
        regulator
   (The value of money should be linked to a real
        commodity)
     Modus ponens. Valid

-68-

8. If epidemiological studies gave us any hint that
         insects played a role in spreading AIDS,
         then we would do more detailed studies
   Epidemiological studies have not given any hint...
   (We are not doing more detailed studies)
      Denying the antecedent. Invalid. [One might
consider whether the hypothetical premise is
implicitly an "if and only if" statement, making the
argument valid.]

EXERCISE E. Presupposes the first two sections, though
the third would help. This exercise has the same
function as Exercise H in Chapter 9.
      1. 2
      2. The converse of If p, then q is If q, then p.
It does not follow.
      3. -(p or q) implies -p and -q.
      4. Either p or q implies If -p, then q.
      5. If p, then q implies Either -p or q.

CHAPTER 11

SYLLOGISMS IN ORDINARY REASONING

Contents

Distilling Deductive Arguments: using linguistic and substantive clues to tell whether an argument is categorical, hypothetical, or disjunctive; nonstandard quantifiers, including "only."

Extended Arguments: analyzing chains of deductive arguments.

Comments

This chapter presupposes the previous chapters in Part III. The second section also employs the diagramming technique from Part II, but in such a way that students who have not read Part II should be able to follow it if given a brief explanation in class.

Within the chapter, the second section could be covered without the first, but one would need to explain the logic of "only" as a quantifier, since it is used both in the text and in the exercises.

I do not introduce the term "sorites" in the second section because it applies only to chains of categorical arguments, and I do not see anything special about them: the same principles can be used to analyze chains of disjunctive or hypothetical syllogisms, or chains involving a mixture of elements. But the term could easily be introduced in class in connection with the first two examples.

I do not discuss the dilemma because I found it hard to find examples outside philosophy. As a mixture of disjunctive and hypothetical elements, however, it could easily be introduced in connection with the subsection "Extended Arguments with Elements of Different Types."

EXERCISE A. Presupposes the first section.
1. All occasions on which one feels pride are occasions followed by a fall.

2. All separate educational facilities are unequal.

3. All marriages in which the partners do not love each other are marriages in which the partners will seek love elsewhere.

4. All vigorous minds are curious.

5. If we were faultless, then we would not derive such satisfaction from remarking the faults of others.

6. If one does not know what happened before one was born, then one remains a child.

7. Either you don't think or you don't hit. [This doesn't really capture the meaning of "at the same time." An alternative would be: if you are hitting, you cannot be thinking at the same time.]

8. All science is a refinement of everyday thinking.

9. All occasions on which the people give up their liberties are occasions on which they are acting under some delusion.

EXERCISE B. Presupposes the first section. This exercise asks students to move in the reverse direction--from standard into nonstandard forms--from that emphasized in the text and the other exercises. The students' first efforts will probably be fairly straightforward statements of the argument. Once they have done this, one might get more mileage from the exercise by asking them to embellish, pad, give examples, asides, etc.--turning their passage into something from which one would have to distill the argument.

EXERCISE C. Presupposes the first section. I have cast the arguments below in the way that I thought best captured their logical form, but many of these choices are debatable.

1. (If the gun had been fired from a distance of less than four yards, then there would have been powder blackening on the clothes)
   There was no powder blackening on the clothes
   The gun was fired from a distance of over four yards
   Valid

2. All clowns are people who stand before a crowd and
           gesture wildly to get their attention
   All politicians are people who stand before a crowd
           and gesture wildly to get their attention
   (All politicians are clowns)
       Invalid: undistributed middle

3. All animals who have true hair and produce milk are
           mammals
   All duckbills and spiny anteaters have true hair
           and produce milk
   All duckbills and spiny anteaters are mammals
       Valid

4. (All opinions about things that do not interest one
           are absolutely valueless)
   All unbiassed opinions are opinions about things
           that do not interest one
   All unbiassed opinions are absolutely valueless
       Valid

5. All cases in which an object is accelerating are
           cases in which some force is acting
   All cases of objects falling to Earth are cases in
           which the object is accelerating
   All cases in which an object falls to Earth are
           cases in which some force is acting
       Valid [This analysis works against the
   hypothetical form of the first sentence, but the
   categorical form seems more appropriate for applying a
   general rule to a specific case.]

6. If we had time enough, this coyness would not be a
           crime
   We do not have time enough
   (This coyness is a crime)
       Invalid: denying the antecedent.

7. All groups that (might have) bombed the Marine
           headquarters are groups with subhuman moral
           standards
   The Syrians are a group with subhuman moral
           standards
   The Syrians bombed the Marine headquarters

Invalid: undistributed middle. [There is the
additional problem here of moving from possibility to
actuality, as indicated by the parenthesis in the
major premise.]

8. All cases in which the eye moves without a moving
        target are cases in which saccadic eye
        movements occur
   All cases of reading are cases in which the eye
        moves without a moving target
   All cases of reading are cases in which saccadic
        eye movements occur
        Valid

9. (Either the whole race of mankind is united into
        one society, or it divides into many
        societies)
   The whole race cannot unite into one society
   The whole race divides into many societies
        Valid

10. All events in which heat flows from a higher to a
        lower temperature are events involving a
        gain in entropy
    All interesting or useful events are events in
        which heat flows....
    All interesting or useful events are events
        involving a gain in entropy
        Valid

11. All things necessary for one who commands are
        things pertaining to war
    (All things that a prince studies should be things
        necessary for one who commands)
    All things that a prince studies should be things
        pertaining to war
        Valid

12. All whites who are apologetic of being accused of
        racism and do not want to confront their
        racist thinking are people who say "Some of
        my best friends are black"
    Mr. Mecham is a person who said "Some of my best
        friends are black"
    Mr. Mecham is a white who....

Invalid: undistributed middle

13. If all prediction is scientific, then horserace
        tipsters are scientists
   (Horserace tipsters are not scientists)
   Not all prediction is scientific

   If all science is predictive, then evolutionary
        biologists are not scientists
   (Evolutionary biologists are scientists)
   Not all science is predictive
   Both valid

EXERCISE D. Presupposes the second section—these are
all extended arguments.

1. (All propositions supported by overwhelming
        evidence are true [are likely to be true,
        should be regarded as true])
   Some laws of economics are propositions supported
        by overwhelming evidence
   Some laws of economics are true

   If every law in economics were false, price
        controls would work
   Some laws of economics are true
   Price controls will not work
      Invalid: second step denies the antecedent

2. If the direction of time depends on the expansion
        of the universe, then if the expansion stops
        and the universe contracts, then time will
        reverse direction
   (The direction of time depends on the expansion of
        the universe)
   If the expansion stops and the universe contracts,
        then time will reverse direction
   The expansion will stop and the universe contract
   (Time will reverse direction)
      Valid. [This analysis rests on the assumption
   that the argument does assert the antecedent of the
   first hypothetical statement.]

3. No one who favors government interference in the
        realm of ideas favors liberty
   (All who favor government support for academic
        research favor government interference in
        the realm of ideas)
   No one who favors government support for academic
        research favors liberty
   All liberals favor government support for academic
     research
   No liberal favors liberty
      Valid as stated, though the assumed premise
   necessary to make it valid does not follow from the
   premise that the arguer probably has in mind: all
   government support for research involves government
   interference.

4. All people with licenses are people who have passed
        the test
   All who can drive in this state are people with
        licenses
   All who can drive in this state are people who have
        passed the test
   No illiterate is a person who has passed the test
   No illiterate is a person who can drive in this
        state
     Valid

5. If the colonists received full representation, then
        the existing Parliament would accept a
        diminution of its power
   The existing Parliament would not accept a
        diminution of its power
   The colonists did not receive full representation

   Either the colonists would receive full
        representation or they would rebel
   They did not receive full representation
   They rebelled
     Valid

EXERCISE E. Presupposes the second section. I would
suggest having students work individually or in small
groups. If they work as individuals, each person might
do step (b) on someone else's step (a). A variant on
step (b) would be to have students give an argument

<u>against</u> one of the premises in step (a).

EXERCISE F. Presupposes the second section. Hayek's argument seems clearly directed against Galbraith's first premise. The argument attacks the link between the urgency of a desire (the value of satisfying it by production) and its originality with the consumer. I see two fairly natural ways of laying out the argument:

A. If Galbraith's premise (1) were true, then artistic
       works would not be worth producing
   <u>Artistic</u> works are worth producing
   Galbraith's premise (1) is not true

B. No desire for an artistic product is a desire that
       exists independently of the product
   <u>Some (all)</u> desires for artistic products are
       desires worth satisfying by increased
       production
   Some desires worth satisfying by increased
       production are desires that do not exist
       independently of the product
To show that this argument attacks premise (1), one would have to recast that premise in categorical form: All desires worth satisfying by increased production are desires that exist independently of the product.

EXERCISE G. Presupposes the second section.

1. If appellant's conduct is a nuisance, then it is
       unreasonably noisy
   <u>If appell</u>ant's conduct is unreasonably noisy, then
       it produces noise out of keeping with the
       character of the neighborhood
   If appellant's conduct is a nuisance, then it
       produces noise out of keeping with the
       character of the neighborhood
   <u>Appell</u>ant's conduct does not produce noise out of
       keeping with the character of the
       neighborhood
   Appellant's conduct is not a nuisance
     Valid

2. All people who have confidence in the future have
      an understanding of the nature of God and
      the soul
   All people who have peace of mind have confidence
      in the future
   All people who have peace of mind have an
      understanding of the nature of God and the
      soul
   All happy people have peace of mind
   All happy people have an understanding of the
      nature of God and the soul
      Valid

3. No mortal is infallible and beyond corruption
   All censors are mortals
   No censor is infallible and beyond corruption

   If censors are not infallible and beyond
      corruption, then the decisions of the
      censors cannot be trusted
   Censors are not infallible and beyond corruption
   The decisions of the censors cannot be trusted
      Valid

4. If thou never wast at court, then thou never saw'st
      good manners
   If thou never saw'st good manners, then thy manners
      are wicked
   If thou never wast at court, then thy manners are
      wicked
   If thy manners are wicked, then thou art sinful
   If thou never wast at court, then thou art sinful
   If thou art sinful, then thou art damned
   If thou never wast at court, then thou art damned
   Thou never wast at court
   Thou art damned
      Valid

5. All things that change over time are things that
      have a history
   Science is a thing that changes over time
   Science is a thing that has a history

All things that have a history are legitimate
        subjects for historians
Science is a thing that has a history
Science is a legitimate subject for historians
    Valid

6. If the U.S. reduced its budget deficit, it would
        not sell as many Treasury securities
    If the U.S. did not sell as many Treasury
        securities, then Japanese and German savers
        would invest elsewhere
    If the U.S. reduced its budget deficit, then
        Japanese and German savers would invest
        elsewhere
    If Japanese and German savers invested elsewhere,
        then American consumers would lack the means
        to finance foreign spending
    If the U.S. reduced its budget deficit, then
        American consumers would lack the means to
        finance foreign spending
    If American consumers lacked the means to finance
        foreign spending, the trade deficit would be
        reduced
    If the U.S. reduced its budget deficit, then the
        trade deficit would be reduced
    Valid

7. No thing that cannot be touched by a pin is a thing
        that can touch a pin
    All things that can dance on the head of a pin are
        things that can touch a pin
    No thing that can dance on a head of a pin is a
        thing that cannot be touched by a pin

    All things that lack physical substance are things
        that cannot be touched by the head of a pin
    No thing that can dance on the head of a pin is a
        thing that cannot be touched by a pin
    No thing that can dance on the head of a pin is a
        thing that lacks physical substance
    All angels lack physical substance
    No angel can dance on the head of a pin
    Valid

8. If we find a gene that increases the risk of a
      disease, then we can find what protein the gene
      codes for
   (If we find what protein the gene codes for, then
         we can find what the protein does)
   If we find a gene that increases the risk of a
         disease, then we can find what the protein
         does
   If we find what the protein does, then we can
         understand the basic mechanism of the
         disease
   If we find a gene that increases the risk of a
         disease, then we can understand the basic
         mechanism of the disease
   If we can understand the basic mechanism of the
         disease, then we can develop treatments
   If we find a gene that increases the risk of a
         disease, then we can develop treatments for
         the disease
      Valid

9. All things that act so as always to obtain an end
         ("obtain the best result") are things that
         act for an end
   Some things that lack knowledge are things that act
         so as always to obtain an end
   Some things that lack knowledge are things that act
         for an end

   If some things that lack knowledge act for an end,
         then they are directed by a being endowed
         with knowledge and intelligence
   Some things that lack knowledge act for an end
   Some things are directed by a being endowed with
         knowledge and intelligence
      Valid

10. Some of you are my personal enemies
    None of you are dead
    Some of my personal enemies are not dead

(All people I considered enemies of the state are
    dead)
Some of my personal enemies are not dead
Some of my personal enemies are not people I
    considered enemies of the state
  Valid

11. If we prohibit owners from moving their factories
        and provide tariff protection, we will grant
        unions and management power to hike wages
        and prices
    If we grant unions and managements power to hike
        wages and prices, industries will become
        even more uncompetitive than they are now
    If we prohibit owners from moving their factories
        and provide tariff protection, then
        industries will become even more
        uncompetitive than they are now
    If industries become even more uncompetitive than
        they are now, the pressures for more
        protectionism will increase
      If we prohibit owners from moving their factories
        and provide tariff protection, the pressures
        for more protectionism will increase
    Valid

12. If the constitution is on a level with ordinary
        legislative acts, then it is alterable when
        the legislature pleases to alter it
    If the constitution is alterable when the
        legislature pleases to alter it, then the
        legislative power is illimitable and written
        constitutions are absurd
    If the constitution is on a level with ordinary
        legislative acts, then the legislative power
        is illimitable and written constitutions are
        absurd
    (The legislative power is not illimitable and
        written constitutions are not absurd)
    The constitution is not on a level with ordinary
        legislative acts

Either the constitution is a supreme paramount law
       or it is on a level with ordinary
       legislative acts
The constitution is not on a level with ordinary
       legislative acts
The constitution is a supreme paramount law
  Valid

13. All things that are mixed with one's labor are
       mixed with a thing that one owns
  All things that are altered from their natural
       state through one's labor are things mixed
       with one's labor
  All things that are altered from their natural
       state through one's labor are mixed with a
       thing one owns

  All things that are mixed with a thing that one
       owns are things that one owns
  All things that are altered from their natural
       state through one's labor are things mixed
       with a thing one owns
  All things that are altered from their natural
       state through one's labor are things one
       owns
  Valid

CHAPTER 12

INDUCTIVE GENERALIZATIONS

Contents

Generalizing: the need to support universal propositions; negative and positive instances; hasty generalization; three rules: vary the sample, look for negative instances, consider plausibility.

Causality: necessary and sufficient conditions; no Practice Quiz.

Agreement and Difference: Mill's methods of agreement and difference (and joint method); negative use of the methods to reject a causal claim; problems in choosing which factors to consider.

Concomitant Variations and Residues: Mill's methods of concomitant variations and residues; strengths and weaknesses of each method.

Comments

This chapter does not presuppose earlier chapters in any strong sense. But if one has not covered Part II (Chapter 5 in particular), one will probably have to spend some time in class discussing logical strength as an inductive analogue of deductive validity. If one has not covered Part III, students may have some questions about the first few pages of the first section, where I relate generalizations to deductive reasoning.

Within the chapter, it would be possible to skip the first section and cover just causality and Mill's methods, though I would not recommend it.

This chapter is the basis for the other three chapters in Part IV, but the other three chapters are mutually independent. One could go directly from this chapter to any of the others.

The text discusses negative uses of the methods of agreement and difference to reject causal claims. Concomitant variations and residues can also be put to a negative use. These are not discussed in the text because I felt a general formulation would be too complicated. But Exercise D, #4 is best seen as a case

of negative variation, so one might want to discuss
this in class.

EXERCISE A. Presupposes the first section. The
generalizations here are of different types, and are
designed to focus attention on various rules and
issues of evaluation.

Like most stereotypes, (1) and (2) are clearly
false, and it's easy to find disconfirming instances.
One might go beyond this to consider why the
stereotypes exist, asking what gives them whatever
degree of initial plausibility they have for some
people.

(3) and (7) are generalizations from folk
psychology, motivational (3) and cognitive (7). Once
again students will probably be able to find
disconfirming instances. Some students may try to save
the generalizations by turning them into something
like tautologies: if absence doesn't make the heart
grow fonder, that only proves the heart wasn't fond to
begin with; if it isn't obvious in retrospect, it
wasn't a true insight. A similar issue arises with
(5): it there's no fatal flaw, it isn't tragic drama.
To avoid circularity, one needs some criterion for
membership in $\underline{S}$ that is independent of $\underline{P}$.

(4), (6), and (8) are generalizations about human
behavior. Given the complexity of behavior, these
can't be true as absolute, single factor explanations.
One might consider whether they can be understood as
statements of contributing factors with implicit
ceteris paribus clauses.

EXERCISE B. Presupposes the third and fourth sections.
Since students will have to decide which factors must
be varied, this is a good occasion for discussing the
plausibility considerations mentioned in the text, as
well as any others one wants to add.

EXERCISE C. This is an integrative exercise,
presupposing Part III as well as the first section of
this chapter. Comparing deductive and inductive
arguments that have the same conclusion is a good way
to focus attention on the differences in the character
of the reasoning. If students come up with good

deductive arguments, one might discuss whether and to what extent these affect the plausibility judgments they bring to bear on the inductive evidence. I have provided some examples of possible deductive arguments below.

1. If one knows a person well, one sees all his flaws, and if one sees all the flaws, one feels contempt.

2. A society is stable only if a large number of people depend on the continuing existence of its rules for acquiring and maintaining wealth, and that happens only when a large number of people support themselves at a comfortable standard of living through their own work--i.e., only if there is a large middle class.

3. People who fear confrontation feel reluctant to express anger; those who are reluctant to express anger feel threatened by feelings of anger toward those who wrong them; those who feel threatened by such feelings are eager to forgive.

4. All narrative literature requires a plot, and you can't have a plot without conflict.

EXERCISE D. Presupposes the third and fourth sections.

1. Effect: no pigeons. Cause: plastic owls. Method: agreement, used to support the causal claim. There is also an implicit use of difference in the final contrast with conditions a month ago.

2. Effect: high sales of Japanese cars in America. Cause: the dollar's high exchange rate. Method: difference, used to reject the causal claim:
1980s: high exchange rate, b, c,... → high sales
1970s: low exchange rate, b, c,... → high sales

3. Effect: infants' attention, interest. Cause: speech sounds. Method: difference, used to support the causal claim.

4. Effect: success of a play. Cause: critics' reviews of plays. Method: concomitant variations, used to reject the causal claim:
"Marilyn": highly negative reviews → lasted a week
"Brothers": mildly negative reviews → lasted one night

5. Effect: reproductive span of cells [in terms of the experiment itself, the effect that is present or absent is the 30 divisions that separate the capacities of embryo and adult cells]. Cause: nucleus. Method: joint, used to support causal claim:
Adult nucleus, adult cell body ———→ 20 divisions
Adult nucleus, embryo cell body ——→ 20 divisions
Embryo nucleus, adult cell body ——→ 50 divisions
Embryo nucleus, embryo cell body ——→ 50 divisions

6. Effect: consumer spending. Cause: rise in stock and bond prices. Method: residues, used to support causal claim: income (presumably wages) obviously explains some part of consumer's willingness to spend, but the difference between 1984 and 1985 shows that income explains only part of that willingness; part must also be due to the other factor.

7. Effect: hares' aversion to eating stems. Cause: pinosylvin methyl ether (PME). Method: joint, used to support causal claim:
Stems: nutritious substances———→ hares eat
Catkins: PME, nutritious substances —┼→ hares eat
Buds: PME, nutritious substances —┼→ hares eat
Oatmeal: nutritious substances,
                        pleasant taste ——→ hares eat
Oatmeal: PME, nutritious substances,
                        pleasant taste —┼→ hares eat

8. Effect: desire to decorate. Cause: desire to highlight things that are attractive in themselves. Method: agreement, used to support causal claim. Chesterton's argument might also be seen as a negative use of difference to reject that claim that decoration is motivated by a desire to hide what is ugly. In either case, it is stretching things a bit to view this as a use of Mill's methods; one might argue that Chesterton is merely providing counterexamples to a generalization.

9. Effect: manic symptoms. Cause: aspartame used in conjunction with antidepressants. Method: joint, used to support causal claim.

10. Effect: terrorist acts against a nation. Cause: nation's prior role in massacres. Method: agreement, used to reject causal claim.

11. Effect: attribution of responsibility. Cause: inner choice. Method: joint, used to support causal claim:
Normal case: inner choice, overt act ———→ responsible
Robot: overt act —|→ responsible
Frustrated
   intention: inner choice,   ———→ responsible

12. Effect: images on photographic plate. Cause: radioactivity. Method: agreement, used to support causal claim. The experiment is also a negative use of difference to reject the claim that X-rays induced by sunlight were the cause of the images.
   i: radioactivity, sunlight ———→ images
  ii: radioactivity   ———→ images

13. Effect: mental states. Cause: proximate neural events. Method: joint, used to support causal claim. The argument is also a joint use of negative agreement and negative difference to reject the claim that the external object is the cause.
Normal: neural event, external object→mental event
Anaesthesia: external event +→ mental event
Dream: neural event,   —→ mental event

CHAPTER 13

ARGUMENT BY ANALOGY

Contents

Analogy and Similarity: distinction between the use of analogies in argument and explanatory or descriptive uses; the role of similarity in an argument by analogy.

Analysis and Evaluation: a method of resolving such arguments into deductive and inductive steps; isolating the relevant dimensions of similarity; ways to challenge an argument by analogy.

Comments

This chapter presupposes Chapter 12, as well as the chapters on the categorical syllogism.

The method of analysis I have developed and presented here rests on the assumption that an argument by analogy acquires whatever strength it has from an implicit generalization, and is not an argument directly from particular to particular. This is a controversial assumption, and I based the entire chapter on it, departing from my usual practice. If I did not accept the assumption, I would not have covered this material, because I think most students are already very good in dealing with arguments by analogy, and I don't know of any other method that would help improve their skills. In any case, those who reject the assumption may want to skip the chapter--though the exercises can probably be put to some use.

Some analogies seem to function as a way of getting the audience to see a phenomenon in a new perspective. When this occurs in the context of persuasion, it is not a purely descriptive or explanatory analogy, yet it does not fit my analysis. The reference to A serves only to draw attention to a fact about B that is then taken as self-evident. No wider generalization need be involved; indeed, strictly speaking there is no argument at all. In Exercise B, items 3, 4, and 7 may be examples of this.

All the exercises presuppose the chapter as a whole.

EXERCISE A. This is an active exercise. Students may come up with any number of different analogies; I've listed below the ones I had in mind in choosing the examples. A possible variant on this exercise would be to have students work individually or in small groups to create the argument, then give the argument to another person or group for analysis; one can then compare the analysis with the original intent.

1. Analogy with Jaguar, Corvette, etc.
2. Analogy with other professions or service industries.
3. Analogy with Vietnam.
4. Analogy with Ronald Reagan.
5. Analogy with plants.

EXERCISE B.

1. Anything subject to malfunction or deterioration should be checked out regularly (at least once a year); the human body is subject....; the human body should be checked out regularly (at least once a year). The plausibility of the argument depends in part on how specific a conclusion regarding the frequency of check-ups the author wants to derive from the analogy with cars. Counter-analogy: the mind is subject to malfunction; should we see a psychiatrist once a year?

2. No preventive measure increases the risk of the harm it is designed to prevent; civil defense preparations are preventive measures; civil defense measures do not increase the risk.... The key question here is whether deterrence requires the maintenance of risk in a way that suspends all analogies with other potential harms.

3. Nothing created to serve a purpose should have extraneous parts; a sentence is created to serve a purpose.... Though an effort of persuasion is clearly being made here, the basis of the analogy may be too vague to count as an argument. No matter how florid, rococo, or redundant a sentence is, couldn't the author claim that everything in it served some

purpose?

4. Any burden has effects that depend on the way the burden is imposed as well as on the absolute magnitude of the burden; taxation is a burden.... The inductive basis is a physical burden borne by a horse; the conclusion concerns a financial burden borne by humans. What happens if we increase the number and variety of instances?

5. Not an argument.

6. No ideologically hostile (and expansive?) nation should be supplied with arms; Khomeini's Iran is an ideologically hostile (and expansive) nation.... The middle term is unclear; the references to fundamentalism and Nazism suggest the role of ideology but there may be other factors intended.

7. Any standard of evaluation must be independent of the things evaluated; moral terms are standards of evaluation.... A possible counter-analogy would be a case where the standard is not independent of the things being measured, but is an extrapolation of an implicit direction of development. E.g., a later draft of a novel may be better than an earlier one because it better actualizes what was only potential before.

8. All combatants who can choose targets at will have an advantage over their opponents; guerrillas are combatants who.... It's hard to deny that the analogy with criminals brings out an advantage of guerrillas. In suggesting that they have the advantage on net, however, the passage is vulnerable to counter-analogies showing the advantages possessed by the government.

9. Any policy of insuring an actual case of a potential harm will increase costs to other policyholders; insuring people with pre-existing medical conditions is a policy of insuring an actual case.... Since the major premise and the conclusion are virtually guaranteed by the mathematics of probability, the analogy with burning buildings may be better interpreted as explanatory, or else as a premise in an implicit argument about fairness.

10. Any coercive arrangement that requires one person to work a specified amount of time for another's purposes is wrong; taxation on earnings is a coercive arrangement that.... The key question here is the relevance of the differences between forced labor

and income taxes--e.g., the conditional nature of the tax (it applies only if one chooses to work), exerting control over the product of labor versus controlling the labor itself.

11. Not an argument.

12. No science can make progress by personifying its objects of study; psychology is (would like to be) a science.... The obvious difference to consider is the nature of the objects: personifying persons may be appropriate even if personifying inanimate things or plants is not.

EXERCISE C. The point here is to indicate how deeply analogies are woven into some of our fundamental conceptions. I've given the counter-analogies I had in mind. Once one has some set of counter-analogies on the table, one might discuss what basic features of society, emotions, and knowledge the opposing analogies bring out, and which features are more essential.

1. Growth, self-actualization, or anything that does not necessarily involve competition.

2. Any non-hydraulic system, such as a computer.

3. Anything suggesting greater individual autonomy and/or competition. To a certain extent, (1) and (3) are counter-analogies to each other.

4. Clouds, nebulas, ships at sea.

EXERCISE D. This is an extended version of Exercise B, in which the analogy and counter-analogy are stated at length.

The deductive element in (1) might best be broken down into two steps, beginning with the respective major premises: i) Anything whose parts are adjusted to each other ... is a machine; ii) All machines are produced by an intelligent being.

CHAPTER 14

STATISTICAL REASONING

Contents

Logic and Statistics: introductory comments; concepts of variable and value. No Practice Quiz.

Using Statistics in Argument: five basic types of statistic (totals, ratios, frequencies, frequency distributions, averages), and the issues to consider in using each type in reasoning.

Statistical Generalization: generalizing from a random sample, sample size and margin of error, biasses in choosing and testing samples.

Statistical Evidence of Causality: correlation and causality, statistical uses of Mill's methods, experiments and observational studies, internal and external validity.

Comments

The first two sections do not presuppose anything earlier in Parts III or IV. It would help if the students had read Chapter 2, but this is not strictly necessary. The third and fourth sections presuppose Chapter 12 but not 13.

This chapter is written for the student who has not had a course in statistics. It provides a conceptual understanding of the numbers, but not the techniques for computing them. Students who have had statistics will find it pretty elementary.

In the fourth section, I analyze statistical evidence of causality in terms of Mill's methods of difference and concomitant variations. In both cases, one might claim that agreement is also involved, since the experimental group is a group containing more than one individual. I would reject the view on the grounds that the effect rarely occurs in every member of the group; what matters is the frequency of the effect in the group as a whole. Such arguments seem to work by treating the group as a single unit having certain statistical properties as a unit.

EXERCISE A. Presupposes the second section.
1. Compatible.
2. Depends on how much imprecision is allowed by the word "about." An order of magnitude seems a bit much.
3. Compatible.
4. Incompatible (assuming the 4 point system).
5. Compatible.

EXERCISE B. Presupposes the second section. All of these involve judgment calls; if they are done in class discussion, I would try to bring out the advantages and disadvantages of each number.
1. My choice would be (c). Expenditures in a single year (a) may be subject to temporary fluctuations. (b) is widely used in political debates, but it does not seem relevant unless we are specifically comparing the importance of the military in the two countries.
2. My choice would be (c). An adjustment for inflation is clearly required; but I see no reason to adjust for changes in median income.
3. It is notoriously difficult to compare costs in private and public education, since they do not really operate in a single market. In the first column, I would pick median tuition at nonreligious schools, since teachers at religious schools rarely earn anywhere near the going rate. For public schools, I would choose average expenditures; fees charged to families outside the district may not bear any relation to costs.
4. None of these numbers is entirely satisfactory. Since only married people can divorce, (a) and (c) could be misleading; they might reflect some change in the number of marriages. The problem with (b) is that those getting married at present and those getting divorced probably belong to different age cohorts. The ideal figure would be the number of divorces as a percentage of all married couples, but I have never seen this number.
5. Everything here depends on what kind of satisfaction one is looking for. (c) is probably the most reasonable measure for the nonprofessional investor, since everyone has the option of putting

money in an interest-yielding instrument; (d) ignores the element of risk.

EXERCISE C. This is an integrative exercise, presupposing Chapter 5 as well as the second section of this chapter, though one might forego the exercise in diagramming and consider only the strength of the inferences. The third section of the chapter would help with some of the items.

1. The conclusion that the government should spend more money on Alzheimer's research may be supported by the statistics in the first paragraph, together with assumptions about the role of government. The statistical comparison with AIDS seems irrelevant, since the cost of research to find the causes of a disease need not be correlated with the number of people who have the disease.

2. To know whether the data in the second sentence support the conclusion in the first, one would need to know whether jobs like mining and cutting timber are included under "major industries" (if so, the figure is very hard to believe).

3. The conclusion seems pretty solid.

4. If the criterion for waste is whether a photocopy ends up in the waste basket, it seems arbitrary: copies can have temporary uses. If one has covered the section on statistical generalizations, moreover, one might ask how Accountemps arrived at its estimate that over 100 billion copies are thrown away.

5. The reasoning here doesn't quite add up. The problem in the second paragraph is that the increase in fatalities might reflect an increase in the number of trucks and/or miles driven, a point noted in the third paragraph. But the answer there is irrelevant. The conclusion is about the effect of deregulation on truck safety; what we need to know is truck fatalities per 100 million miles in 1975 versus 1984.

6. If Soviet gross national product greatly increased between 1955 and 1977, the smaller proportion devoted to medicine in 1977 might be a much larger amount in absolute terms. I think one would need both the absolute numbers and the percentages to derive a conclusion about the priority of medical care.

7. One might object here that the two categories of researchers—those supported and those not supported by industry—may not be comparable in talent or productiveness; it may be that the industry-supported ones would have had an even higher academic output if they were not supported. But the conclusion does not say industry support has _no_ effect, merely that it does not lead people to neglect their "faculty duties." So I would say the conclusion is well supported.

8. If the conclusion here is that the elderly as a group are not poor compared to other age groups, the data provide some support, though it would be more convincing to take a single measure—poverty rate, discretionary income, etc.—and compare the elderly to all other age groups. If the conclusion is that government policy unjustly favors the elderly, one would need to know much more even to interpret the numbers given: how much of the discretionary income is earned or results from savings? how much of Social Security income is covered by previous taxes paid (plus interest) and how much is welfare? Etc.

EXERCISE D. Presupposes the chapter as a whole.

1. Pre-BAT 1000: average SAT = x
   Post-BAT 1000: average SAT = x + 12
Very weak: we don't know whether average SAT scores were rising anyway, and a change that small could easily be due to random fluctuations.

2. Families of nondisruptive students: x% of parents
           display irritability
   Families of disruptive students: 3x% of parents
           display irritability
The difference is striking, and one can probably assume it was statistically significant. A tendency to display irritability, however, might easily be confounded with other traits. The intervention described in the last sentence increases the strength of the argument in this regard, turning it from an observational study into something like an experiment.

3. The obvious problem here is the direction of causality: do people oppose the law because they drive faster, or do they drive faster because they oppose the law, or both?

4. Men with younger wives: death rate 13% below
          average
   Men with older wives: death rate 20% over average
The potential for confounding variables here is enormous: differences in health, wealth, vitality, etc., might explain both the lower death rate and attraction to and for younger women. And if there is a direct causal connection, it's conceivable that it runs in the opposite direction: younger women may be more attracted to older men whom they expect to live longer.

5. Cognitive behavior patients: 50–60% recovery
   Interpersonal patients: 50–60% recovery
   Drug patients: 50–60% recovery
   Placebo patients: 30% recovery
I would say the evidence for causality is strong. It is an experiment rather than an observational study, a placebo was used, and experimental and control groups were chosen randomly.

6. As noted in the text, this inference is weakened by the possibility of confounding variables: differences in intelligence, ambition, family social status, etc., may explain both the pursuit of a college degree and the higher earnings.

7. To make the causal inference clear, one needs to compare the votes of those who received NRA money and votes of those who did not—information that is not stated but can be calculated:
   Members who received NRA funds (233): 85% voted for
          law
   Members who didn't get funds (191): 18% voted for
          law
The obvious problem is the direction of causality: it may be that the NRA gave funds primarily to those who were already inclined—out of conviction or whatever— to support the law.

8. A rise in immune-system function is attributed to three different factors altogether: fantasies of selfless love, watching a film of Mother Teresa, and thoughts of loving and being loved. In each case, there is a potential for confounding variables: perhaps the immune system change was a result of some feeling--e.g., inspiration, relaxation--that is itself caused by love but might also be caused by other feelings or thoughts. In addition, the definition of selfless love in McKay's research (as reported) includes a sense of humor and lack of cynicism, which are not part of love per se in ordinary terms; and the use of fantasies as a proxy variable for actual selfless love is questionable.

EXERCISE E. Presupposes the chapter as a whole. This can be an integrative exercise if one uses the diagram technique for debates (Chapter 7). Even if one doesn't do the diagrams, the debate format should encourage students to think at two levels. In constructing arguments for their own position, they must use the statistical information as premises. In attacking the opposite position (and defending their own against attacks), they will have to question the basis of the statistics, using what they've learned in the third and fourth sections. If one is doing this in class, I would suggest having students actually take sides.

Some of the statistics could be used to support either conclusion. (1) could be taken--in conjunction with (2)--as evidence of the magnitude of the danger from guns, or as evidence of the magnitude of the intrusion a gun control law would entail. (4) could be taken as a reason for prohibiting the homicidally-inclined from having guns, or as a reason for seeing the homicidal inclinations as the problem rather than the guns per se.

Items (2) and (5) come from activist, lobbying organizations. This raises questions of credibility, even if one resists the temptation to poison the well completely. If one is going to spend some time on this, students might be encouraged to try to find confirmation of the numbers from more neutral sources.

One could expand the exercise by adding items to the list, by having students do research to find additional information, or by having them make lists of additional information they would like to have.

CHAPTER 15

EXPLANATION

Contents

Explanation and Argument: hypothesis and explanandum, diagramming explanations.

Adequacy: three standards for evaluating the internal adequacy of an explanation: strength of the inference from hypothesis to explanandum, completeness, and informativeness.

The Truth of Hypotheses: testing a hypothesis by inferring further consequences from it; auxiliary assumptions; using consistency and simplicity in making plausibility judgments.

Comments

This chapter is built around a set of structural analogies between arguments and explanations— analogies between premises and hypotheses, conclusions and explananda, logical strength and internal adequacy, the truth of the premises and the truth of hypotheses. The same diagrams used to analyze arguments are used to analyze the internal structure of explanations. This is not a product of any specific view about the nature of explanation, and I believe the method of analysis can be used by people with different views on that subject. The primary purpose of the analogy is pedagogical: to simplify things for students by using what they already know from studying argument analysis.

In this respect, the chapter bears a strong connection with Chapter 5. The diagramming technique is explained fully enough, however, that students who have not read Chapter 5 should be able to follow.

The chapter makes some references to specific forms of inductive and deductive arguments, but not enough to make anything in Parts III or IV a strong presupposition. A course concentrating on argument analysis could go directly from Part II to this chapter.

EXERCISE A. Presupposes the first section. The exercise does not ask students to supply implicit premises, and I have not done so below, but one might do this as an extension of the exercise.

1. 1) A zygote obtains half its genes from its male parent
   2) A zygote receives half its chromosomes from its male parent
   3) The chromosomes bear the genes

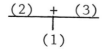

2. 1) Israel's diplomatic isolation is easing
   2) The power of Arab oil-producing countries is declining
   3) The price of oil has slipped
   4) Prime Minister Peres has projected a more moderate image for Israel

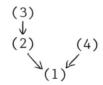

3. 1) Blisters can form on the skin
   2) When the skin is subject to friction, the upper layers move back and forth over the lower layers
   3) When the layers move, a small cleft is produced
   4) When a cleft is produced, fluid collects in the cleft
   5) When the skin is burned, serum from damaged blood vessels collects between epidermis and dermis

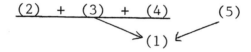

4. 1) Wrought iron is soft and tough
   2) Cast iron is hard and brittle
   3) Steel is moderately hard and moderately tough
   4) The hardness and toughness of a metal extracted
      from iron ore is determined by its carbon
      content
   5) Wrought iron has a carbon content of 0-.15%
   6) Cast iron has a carbon content of 1.5% or more
   7) Steel has a carbon content of .15-1.5%

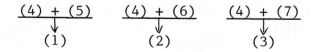

This analysis does not fully capture all the
relationships explained by the chemical model. This is
a problem with viewing explanation exclusively in
terms of propositions, and the example might be the
occasion for commentary on the role of models in
science.

5. 1) Many free-swimming animals are silvery white on
      their bellies
   2) Seen from below, the shining white belly blends
      perfectly with the reflecting surface of the
      water
   3) Animals with white bellies are invisible to
      predators in the depths

This explanation clearly presupposes an evolutionary
framework. An interesting exercise would be to
formulate the weakest premise regarding adaptation
that is strong enough to cover the inference from (3)
to (1).

6. 1) When a can of spherical objects of different sizes is shaken, the larger objects end up on the surface
   2) When a void opens during shaking, it is more likely to be filled by a small than a large object
   3) For a large object to move down, several small objects must move out of the way simultaneously
   4) For one or more small objects to move down, only one large object must move out of the way

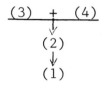

$$\frac{(3) \ + \ (4)}{}$$
$$\downarrow$$
$$(2)$$
$$\downarrow$$
$$(1)$$

I have used the term "objects" to allow generalization from balls to nuts.

7. 1) Overall prosperity has continued despite weakness in manufacturing industries
   2) Service sector jobs have increased
   3) Service sector jobs are relatively safe from business cycles and layoffs

$$\frac{(2) \ + \ (3)}{}$$
$$\downarrow$$
$$(1)$$

EXERCISE B. Presupposes the second section.

1. This seems logically weak, a) since it isn't clear that people in decision-making positions set musical trends, and b) since those people will be in those positions for some time, after the fad has ended.

2. This seems reasonably adequate to me. It might be challenged on grounds of fundamentality, since it assumes without explanation that political authorities would naturally want control over things causing scandal or major controversy.

3. I would say this is circular. The explanandum is that in a tie, the runner is not ruled out. The hypothesis is that the defense has not discharged its responsibilty to put the runner out. This doesn't tell

us what should count as putting the runner out. The defense could have the responsibility attributed to it even if the rule were that the runner loses a tie.

EXERCISE C. Presupposes the first section. The exercise is intended to encourage students to read newspapers more critically. An extension of the exercise would be to have students look for further examples of this phenomenon, which is quite common in journalism.

    1. Hypothesis: Margaret Thatcher reduced income taxes in order to increase her chances of reelection. Alternative: Thatcher believed the cut would help the country.

    2. Reagan expelled the Soviet diplomats in an effort to look tough during the Daniloff affair. Alternative: Reagan acted to protect national security.

    3. Hypothesis: The House acted under the influence of organized labor. Alternative: The House acted from a sense of justice.

EXERCISE D. This is an active exercise, presupposing the chapter as a whole. If it is being done in class, one might see how many alternative explanations students can come up with. If they work individually or in groups, they might give their explanations to others for criticism regarding adequacy and testing design.

EXERCISE E. This is a comic interlude, intended to promote discussion about plausibility judgments. I have grouped the headlines into categories and ranked the categories in decreasing order by consistency. As an extension, one might have students look for other headlines of this type, competing to see who can find the least plausible one.

    Coincidences that do not involve any physical improbability: 6, 8

    Events that are physically unlikely but can be explained by existing knowledge: 1

    Events which cannot be explained by existing knowledge, but might be explained by new principles that do not conflict with existing knowledge: 4, 10, 5, 7

Events whose occurrence would conflict with existing knowledge: 2, 3, 9

EXERCISE F. Presupposes the chapter as a whole. The point here is to have students work out on a really bad example of explanation, where the flaws are writ large. If it is done in class, one person or group might be assigned the role of Zero, trying to save the hypothesis about GM's computers by rejecting auxiliary assumptions and inventing new wrinkles in the hypothesis.

EXERCISE G. Presupposes the chapter as a whole. This exercise complements the previous one. The hypothesis (that Hatchett is guilty) is not outlandish but quite plausible; indeed, through the end of the second paragraph it seems irresistible. A further advantage is that the Appeals Court explicitly uses the framework of propositions to be proved and alternative hypotheses. One way to start discussion is to ask how many students think Hatchett is guilty, and then ask how many would vote to convict him were they on the jury. Students who vote yes on the first but not the second question can be asked to explain why.